KILL ....
NEIGHBOUR

by Lucie Lovatt

‖SAMUEL FRENCH‖

Copyright © 2024 by Lucie Lovatt
Cover artwork © 2024 Rebecca Pitt
All Rights Reserved

KILL THY NEIGHBOUR is fully protected under the copyright laws of the British Commonwealth, including Canada, the United States of America, and all other countries of the Copyright Union. All rights, including professional and amateur stage productions, recitation, lecturing, public reading, motion picture, radio broadcasting, television, online/digital production, and the rights of translation into foreign languages are strictly reserved.

ISBN 978-0-573-00051-5

concordtheatricals.co.uk
concordtheatricals.com

FOR AMATEUR PRODUCTION ENQUIRIES

UNITED KINGDOM AND WORLD
EXCLUDING NORTH AMERICA
licensing@concordtheatricals.co.uk
020-7054-7298

Each title is subject to availability from Concord Theatricals, depending upon country of performance.

CAUTION: Professional and amateur producers are hereby warned that *KILL THY NEIGHBOUR* is subject to a licensing fee. The purchase, renting, lending or use of this book does not constitute a licence to perform this title(s), which licence must be obtained from the appropriate agent prior to any performance. Performance of this title(s) without a licence is a violation of copyright law and may subject the producer and/or presenter of such performances to penalties. Both amateurs and professionals considering a production are strongly advised to apply to the appropriate agent before starting rehearsals, advertising, or booking a theatre. A licensing fee must be paid whether the title is presented for charity or gain and whether or not admission is charged.

This work is published by Samuel French, an imprint of Concord Theatricals Ltd.

For inquiries about the Professional Rights in this play, contact Concord Theatricals.

No one shall make any changes in this title for the purpose of production. No part of this book may be reproduced, stored in a retrieval system, scanned, uploaded, or transmitted in any form, by any means, now known or yet to be invented, including mechanical, electronic, digital, photocopying, recording, videotaping, or otherwise, without the prior written permission of the publisher. No one shall share this title, or part of this title, to any social media or file hosting websites.

The moral right of Lucie Lovatt to be identified as author of this work has been asserted in accordance with Section 77 of the Copyright, Designs and Patents Act 1988.

USE OF COPYRIGHTED MUSIC

A licence issued by Concord Theatricals to perform this play does not include permission to use the incidental music specified in this publication. In the United Kingdom: Where the place of performance is already licensed by the PERFORMING RIGHT SOCIETY (PRS) a return of the music used must be made to them. If the place of performance is not so licensed then application should be made to PRS for Music (www.prsformusic.com). A separate and additional licence from PHONOGRAPHIC PERFORMANCE LTD (www.ppluk.com) may be needed whenever commercial recordings are used. Outside the United Kingdom: Please contact the appropriate music licensing authority in your territory for the rights to any incidental music.

USE OF COPYRIGHTED THIRD-PARTY MATERIALS

Licensees are solely responsible for obtaining formal written permission from copyright owners to use copyrighted third-party materials (e.g., artworks, logos) in the performance of this play and are strongly cautioned to do so. If no such permission is obtained by the licensee, then the licensee must use only original materials that the licensee owns and controls. Licensees are solely responsible and liable for clearances of all third-party copyrighted materials, and shall indemnify the copyright owners of the play(s) and their licensing agent, Concord Theatricals Ltd., against any costs, expenses, losses and liabilities arising from the use of such copyrighted third-party materials by licensees.

The prologue is adapted from Dylan Thomas' *Under Milk Wood* (1954), which is in the public domain in the United Kingdom.

IMPORTANT BILLING AND CREDIT REQUIREMENTS

If you have obtained performance rights to this title, please refer to your licensing agreement for important billing and credit requirements.

NOTE

This programme text was produced from a rehearsal draft of the script, and may differ from the final production.

Theatr Clwyd

The award-winning **Theatr Clwyd** is Wales' biggest producing theatre. Since 1976 Theatr Clwyd has created exceptional theatre from its home in Flintshire, North Wales. Driven by the vision and dynamism of Executive Director Liam Evans-Ford and newly appointed Artistic Director Kate Wasserberg, Theatr Clwyd pushes theatrical boundaries creating world-class productions.

In 2021, Theatr Clwyd was named as *The Stage*'s 'Regional Theatre Of The Year'. Major recent successes have included co-producing *The Famous Five: A New Musical* with Chichester Festival Theatre; *Home, I'm Darling* with the National Theatre, which won Best New Comedy at the Olivier Awards and was nominated in five categories; the UK Theatre Award-winning musical *The Assassination of Katie Hopkins*; the site-specific, immersive *Great Gatsby* and the Menier Chocolate Factory co-production of *Orpheus Descending*.

Theatr Clwyd is one of only four theatres in the UK to build sets and props, make costumes and paint scenery in-house. Their impressive team of workshop, wardrobe and scenic artists, props makers and technicians ensure the skills vital to a vibrant theatre industry are nurtured right in the heart of Wales, developing the theatremakers of the future. In addition to this, Theatr Clwyd hosts an artist development programme, trainee technicians' scheme and an eighteen-month traineeship for directors and designers, to develop the Artistic Directors of the future.

Theatr Clwyd works in the community across all art forms and is recognised as a cultural leader for its cross generational theatre groups, work in youth justice and diverse programme of arts, health and wellbeing. Award-winning Community Engagement projects include 'Arts from the Armchair', in partnership with Betsi Cadwaladr University Health Board, which uses theatrical-making skills to help people with early onset memory loss and their carers; and 'Justice In A Day', working in schools and the law courts to help at-risk children to realise the consequences of crime.

Theatr Clwyd Music was established in 2020, adopting the council-run Flintshire Music Service to ensure that this vital community asset wasn't lost and could grow and flourish. Providing music lessons throughout schools and community settings for all ages, the team has now grown to over thirty musicians.

In 2022, Theatr Clwyd took over the running and programming of William Aston Hall, Wrexham, in partnership with Wrexham University. Together they are protecting this vital arts venue as a community asset, ensuring that the people of Wrexham and North Wales have access to the best in Welsh, UK and International Entertainment.

The **Torch Theatre** is a creative force in west Wales with long-standing national significance and an international reputation. The centre for the arts in Pembrokeshire, the Torch was established in 1977 and is one of three key producing houses in Wales.

Led by Executive Director Benjamin Lloyd and Artistic Director Chelsey Gillard, the Torch prioritises the development of Welsh and Wales-based artists and freelancers through our broad artistic programme and engagement opportunities for all in our community, from our award-winning in-house theatrical productions to the delivery of an expansive creative engagement programme.

Our offer includes over 2,000 events each year with activities reaching over 100,000 people from our base in Pembrokeshire and across the UK via our touring productions and through Sunset Cinema, our outdoor summer cinema programme which visits some of Pembrokeshire's and South Wales' most iconic locations. In our 300 seat Main House, our 102 seat Studio Theatre, our fine art gallery and our accessible front of house spaces including Café Torch, we invite people to come and enjoy our homemade productions each year. These include new writing, classic adaptations and our original pantomime, and are supported by a rich visiting programme that includes drama, comedy, live music, ballet, dance, family shows, live broadcasts, opera and new work. We are also a cinema, screening a mix of the latest blockbusters and independent films. Initiatives such as our relaxed performances, dementia-friendly screenings (Movies and Memories) and Babies and Blockbusters, ensure that our programme and building are open to everyone.

The Torch is equally a vital community resource, delivering life-enriching experiences from our prominent position on the skyline of Milford Haven. Our vibrant Youth & Community department provides creative engagement opportunities for all, including Youth Theatre for young people aged seven to eighteen, Torch Voices community choir, Coffi Cymraeg (our monthly Welsh learners coffee morning) and a host of adult skills classes. Alongside this we offer an extensive range of opportunities for our educational partners, including bespoke workshops and teacher training.

The Torch Theatre is a limited company with charitable status and is a publicly funded theatre supported by Arts Council of Wales, the Welsh Government, Pembrokeshire County Council and Milford Haven Town Council. We are also generously supported by local businesses including Milford Haven Port Authority.

www.torchtheatre.co.uk

ACKNOWLEDGEMENTS

Thank you to all the teams at Theatr Clwyd.

Thank you to the dedicated staff and volunteer teams at Torch Theatre and to the Torch Theatre Board of Management.

Thank you to all the funders and supporters of Theatr Clwyd.

The Torch acknowledges the support of our principal funders and that of our business, community and education partners across Wales.

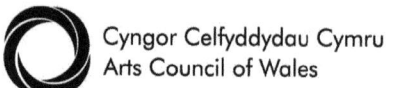

AUTHOR'S ACKNOWLEDGEMENTS

Thank you to the brilliant teams at both Theatr Clwyd and Torch Theatre, especially Chelsey Gillard and Kate Wasserberg.

Thank you to the supportive tutors and students I worked closely with at Bristol Old Vic Theatre School during the early life of this play, especially Stephanie Dale, David Edgar and James Peries.

Thank you to my partner Owen Phillips for his endless support and inspiration.

Thank you to David Lovatt and Sandra Lovatt for being such loving parents.

Thank you also to Jack Bradley, Sally Cookson, Branwen Davies, Claire Etherington, Georgia Gatti, Indeg Gonzalez-Thomas, Tamara Harvey, Ioan Hefin, Helen James, Gabin Kongolo, Kyle Lima, Raphael Martin, Julia Meadwell, Bethan Morgan, Rhodri Morgan, Farlane Namuyamba-Lovatt, Rhiannon Oliver, Glyn Richards, Lydia Rynne, Clêr Stephens, Jâms Thomas, Seren Vickers, Rick Yale and the team at Samuel French and Concord Theatricals.

Special thanks to Nye and Stella for making me want to grow again.

KILL THY NEIGHBOUR was first produced by Theatr Clwyd and the Torch Theatre, and premiered at Theatr Clwyd on 2nd April 2024. The cast (in order of appearance) and company were as follows:

GARETH . . . . Jamie Redford
CARYL . . . . Victoria John
MAX . . . . Gus Gordon
MEIRION . . . . Dafydd Emyr
SEREN . . . . Catrin Stewart

Writer . . . . Lucie Lovatt
Director . . . . Chelsey Gillard
Set & Costume Designer . . . . Elin Steele
Lighting Designer . . . . Lucía Sánchez Roldán
Composer & Sound Designer . . . . Tic Ashfield
Intimacy Director . . . . Bethan Eleri
Assistant Director . . . . Ellie Rose
Casting Director . . . . Polly Jerrold
Production Manager . . . . Jim Davis
Wellbeing Facilitator . . . . Hester Evans
Company Stage Manager . . . . Alec Reece
Deputy Stage Manager . . . . Tyla Thomas
Assistant Stage Manager . . . . Emma Hardwick
Producer . . . . Jenny Pearce

CAST

GARETH | JAMIE REDFORD
Jamie Redford graduated with a BA in Acting from the Royal Conservatoire Scotland in 2020. TV roles in *Emmerdale* and *Doctors*, and stage credits include *Road* with Taking Flight Theatre Company. Jamie has co-written a television pilot currently in pre-production. Jamie has written and is set to perform in a one-man show, touring later this year, reflecting his Welsh valleys upbringing.

CARYL | VICTORIA JOHN
Theatre credits include: *Truth or Dare, Celebrated Virgins, Pavilion, Wave Me Goodbye, Cyrano de Bergerac, All My Sons, The Light of Heart, Aristocrats, The Winslow Boy, Rape of the Fair Country, Boeing Boeing, Roots, The Suicide, A Chorus of Disapproval* (Theatr Clwyd); *Glitterball* (RifCo Theatre); *HIR* (Bush Theatre); *Play/Silence* (The Other Room); *The Frozen Scream* (WMC/Birmingham Hippodrome); *Cancer Time* (the Caramel Club); *Never, Fear, Love?* (Velvet Ensemble/WMC); *The Gut Girls* (Velvet Ensemble/Sherman Cymru); *Treasure* (King's Head Theatre); *Reasons for Feeling* (Tristan Bates Theatre); *The Bitter Tears of Petra Von Kant* (Flaming Theatre Company) and *The Real Story of Puss in Boots* (Streetwise Fringe, Dubai).

Television: *Gwaith/Cartref* (S4C/Fiction Factory); *Miranda* (BBC); *Cast Offs* (Channel 4) and Rhiannon in *Little Britain* (BBC).

Radio: *Telling the Bees* (BBC Wales).

MAX | GUS GORDON
Originally from Cornwall, Gus moved to London at sixteen to train at the Brit School, before attending Italia Conti on their BA acting program.

Since graduating in 2018, he has appeared in Netflix's *The Sandman* directed by Mike Barker, BBC's *Doctors* and *Eastenders*. He has also appeared as Simon Riffkind in Jeremy Dyson and Andy Nyman's West End production of *Ghost Stories*.

MEIRION | DAFYDD EMYR
Dafydd has been a film, TV, voice and stage actor for over thirty years. His theatre work includes Geppeto in *Pinocchio*, Dad in *Danny The Champion Of The World*, Merlin in *Merlin And The Cave Of Dreams* (Sherman); General Howell in *Kiss Me Kate*, Big Jule in *Guys And Dolls* (Crucible); Michael D Jones/John Evans in *Patagonia 150* (NTW/TGC).

His TV/film work includes *Deryn, Lleifior, Amdani, Dr. Who, Casualty, Excalibur, The Search for Arthur, Pobl Y Cwm, Bastard Executioner, Rebecca's Daughters, Old Scores, Wild Justice*. He's also a stage and radio writer and loves dabbling in poetry.

SEREN | CATRIN STEWART

Theatre credits include: *Hamlet* (Bristol Old Vic); *Hero of the People* (Sherman Theatre); *Valued Friends* (Rose Theatre Kingston); *1984* (West End); *Cat On a Hot Tin Roof* (Theatr Clwyd); *Jew of Malta* and *Love's Sacrifice* (RSC); *The Cherry Orchard* (The Young Vic); *Mametz* and *The Devil Inside Him* (National Theatre of Wales); *Longing* (Hampstead Theatre); *Romeo and Juliet* (Headlong); *Buried Child* (Leicester Curve); *The Lady from the Sea* (The Manchester Royal Exchange).

Television credits include: *Kill list* (Sky); *Doctors, Casualty* (BBC); *Lifelines* (S4C); *Bang* (BAFTA WALES WINNER, S4C/BBC Wales); *Doctor Who* (BBC); *Stella* (Sky One); *Misfits* (E4); *Hearts of Gold* (BBC).

She won Best Performance in a British Feature Award at the Edinburgh Film Festival for 'The Library Suicides' film (BFI/ Ffilm Cymru) directed by Euros Lyn.

She has also worked on many radio productions for BBC Radio 4 and audio series for Big Finnish, as well as award-winning short films.

COMPANY

WRITER | LUCIE LOVATT

Lucie has recently reignited her writing ambitions and, following her short *Maternity Leave* playing as part of Theatr Clwyd's Truth/Dare, *Kill Thy Neighbour* is her first full-length play.

Lucie has worked in West End theatre for many years as a creative producer, previously for Sonia Friedman Productions and now for Second Half Productions. Credits include; *Long Day's Journey Into Night, Ulster American, A Mirror, Harry Potter and the Cursed Child, Sunny Afternoon the Musical, Legally Blonde the Musical, All About Eve, The Ferryman, Rosmersholm, Who's Afraid of Virginia Woolf?, Jerusalem, Mojo, Shakespeare in Love, A Christmas Carol, Chimerica* and *Hamlet*.

Lucie is an alumna of the Royal Court Theatre's Young Writers' Programme (Introduction and Invitation) and recently completed an MA in Dramatic Writing at Bristol Old Vic Theatre School.

DIRECTOR | CHELSEY GILLARD

Chelsey is the Artistic Director of the Torch Theatre.

Previously she was the Carne Trust Associate Director at the Stephen Joseph Theatre in Scarborough, where she directed the second company for the world premiere of Sir Alan Ayckbourn's 85th show *The Girl Next Door*. She began her career at The Other Room, Cardiff's pub theatre, initially as Assistant Director, then Associate Director.

She is an Associate Artist of Chippy Lane Productions and is co-founder of PowderHouse Theatre.

Directing credits include: *Private Lives* and *Beauty and The Beast* (Torch Theatre); *Right Where We Left Us* and *BLUE* (Chippy Lane Productions); *Antigone* (co-directed with Jac Ifan Moore, online, for National Theatre Wales, Theatr Genedlaethol Cymru and PowderHouse); *The Invisible Woman* (Welsh tour with Wales Millennium Centre); *Saethu Cwningod/ Shooting Rabbits* (co-directed with Jac Ifan Moore, Sherman Theatre and PowderHouse), *[BLANK]* (Sherman Youth Theatre); *The Burton Taylor Affair* (Sherman Theatre and Oran Mor, Glasgow Lunchtime Theatre); *My Name is Rachel Corrie* (The Other Room and Graphic); *Constellation Street* (co-directed with Dan Jones, The Other Room, winner of Wales Theatre Awards Best Production in the English language).

As Associate or Assistant Director: *The Girl Next Door*, *The Snow Queen*, *Treasure Island* (Stephen Joseph Theatre); *Seanmhair* (The Other Room and Bedlam Edinburgh); *ENGLISH* (National Theatre Wales and Quarantine); *The Weir* (Sherman Theare and Tobacco Factory Theatres); *Cat on a Hot Tin Roof* (Theatr Clwyd and touring); *Blasted* (The Other Room); *A Midsummer Night's Dream* (Pontardawe Arts Centre and touring).

SET & COSTUME DESIGNER | ELIN STEELE

Elin trained in Design for Performance at the Royal Welsh College of Music and Drama. She was a 2019 Linbury Prize Finalist, received the 2020 Royal Opera House Bursary and is a RWCMD Honorary Associate.

Design credits include: *Cinders!* (Scottish Ballet); *Branwen:Dadeni* (WMC/Frân Wen); *A Midsummer Night's Dream* (Sherman Theatre); *The Scandal at Mayerling* (Scottish Ballet); *Anne of Green Gables* (London Children's Ballet); *Passion* (Hope Mill Theatre); *Firebird Reimagined* (McNicol Ballet Collective); *A Hero of the People* (Sherman Theatre); *Faust+Greta* (Theatr Genedlaethol Cymru/Frân Wen); *The Merthyr Stigmatist* (Sherman Theatre/Theatre Uncut); *Why Are People Clapping?* (NDCW); *Llyfr Glas Nebo* (Frân Wen); *Dextera* (Scottish Ballet); *Woof* (Sherman Theatre).

As young associate: *Romeo and Juliet* (Matthew Bourne's New Adventures).

LIGHTING DESIGNER | LUCÍA SÁNCHEZ ROLDÁN

As Lighting Designer, theatre includes: *Wonderful World of Dissocia* (Stratford East); *The Importance of Being Earnest* (Mercury Theatre); *Grate* (National Theatre of Kosovo); *Under Milk Wood* (Sherman Theatre); *The E.U. Killed My Dad* (Jermyn Street Theatre); *Papercut* (Park 90); *How to Succeed in Business Without Really Trying* (Southwark Playhouse Large); *Suddenly, Last Summer* (as Co-Lighting

Designer with Jamie Platt, English Theatre Frankfurt); *Orpheus Descending* (National Theatre of Albania); *We'll Be Who We Are* (Vault Festival); *The Walworth Farce* (Southwark Playhouse Elephant); *Fefu and Her Friends, Not About Nightingales* (Tobacco Factory); *Bogeyman* (Pleasance/Camden's People Theatre); *Black, El Payaso* (Arcola Theatre, Cervantes Theatre); *Camp Albion* (Watermill Theatre); *We Are the Best!* (Live Theatre); *Tapped* (Theatre 503); *The Forest Awakens, Code and Dagger, A New Beginning* (Kiln); *The Gift* (GBS RADA); *Barbarians* (Silk Street); *Everything Must Go* (RnD Playground); *Invisibles, The First* (Vault Festival); *The Spirit* (BAC); *Ms Julie, Utopia Room* (The Place); *The Niceties* (Finborough); *How We Begin* (Kings Head).

As Associate Lighting Designer, theatre includes: *Stranger Things: The First Shadow* (Phoenix Theatre, West End); *Drive Your Plow Over the Bones of the Dead* (Complicité); *two Palestinians go dogging* (Royal Court); *Cabaret* (Playhouse, West End); *Camp Siegfried* (Old Vic); *Taboo Anniversary Concert* (London Palladium); *Mirror and the Light* (Gielgud, West End); *Amélie* (Criterion, West End); *Les Misérables: The Staged Concert* (Sondheim, West End); *Moonlight and Magnolias* (Nottingham Playhouse); *The Fishermen* (West End and Marlowe).

COMPOSER & SOUND DESIGNER | TIC ASHFIELD

Tic Ashfield is a BAFTA Cymru award-winning composer and sound designer who studied at the Royal Welsh College of Music and Drama. Tic trained in creative music technology at undergraduate and then gained a masters degree in composition supported by the Prince of Wales scholarship.

Theatre & Dance work includes: *Meta vs Life* (Hijinx Theatre); *Housemates* (Sherman Theatre, Hijinx Theatre); *Es & Flo* (Wales Millennium Centre, Kiln Theatre); *Pijin/Pigeon* (Theatr Genedlaethol Cymru, Theatr Iolo); *Right Where We Left Us* (Chippy Lane Productions); *The Boy With Two Hearts* (Wales Millennium Centre, National Theatre); *Anthem* (Wales Millennium Centre); *Rocket Launch Blaenavon* (Tin Shed Theatre); *Qwerin* (Osian Meilir); *Ghost Light* (Ffwrnes Theatre); *Pryd Mae'r Haf?* (Theatr Genedlaethol Cymru); *A Number, All But Gone, The Awkward Years, American Nightmare, The Story, Hela* (The Other Room); *The Gathering, {150}, The Tide Whisperer, For As Long As The Heart Beats, Storm III* (National Theatre Wales); *On Bear Ridge* (National Theatre Wales & The Royal Court); *Dear To Me | Annwyl i mi* (National Dance Company Wales); *The Invisible Woman* (Alisa Jenkins); *Peeling* (Taking Flight Theatre); *Blue* (Chippy Lane Productions); *Bottom* (Willy Hudson); *Richard III, Henry VI, Romeo & Juliet* (Omidaze Productions); *Saturday Night Forever* (Joio); *Moment(o)s of Leaving* (Elaine Paton); *Hard Times* (Lighthouse Theatre); *Cold Rolling* (Ballet Cymru); *My People* (Gwyn Emberton Dance); *Tir Sir Gar* (Theatr Genedlaethol Cymru).

Film and television work includes: *Tree On A Hill | Pen Ar Y Bryn* (Fiction Factory/S4C/BBC), *The Light In The Hall* (C4/S4C), *STAD* (S4C), *Bregus* (S4C), *Hel Y Mynydd* (S4C), *Pili Pala* (S4C), *Hidden | Craith* (S4C/BBC), *Hinterland | Y Gwyll* (S4C/BBC), *Galesa* (Joio), *Andrew Marr: Great Scots* (BBC), *The Girl In The Diary* (S4C).

INTIMACY DIRECTOR | BETHAN ELERI

Bethan is an Actor, Stunt Performer, Fight Director and Intimacy Director who trained at East 15 Acting School.

Since graduating she's worked on many projects: from notable productions such as *Enola Holmes 2* and *Misbehaviour*; to prestigious theatres in the UK including the Royal Opera House. She has also worked internationally, including a two-month tour of *Wuthering Heights* across China in some of China's most reputable theatres.

Her work as an Intimacy Director is further informed by both her work as an actor and as a Fight Director. As an experienced actor she has a deep understanding of the actors' needs in vulnerable and intimate moments. Similarly, having professionally choreographed fight scenes for film and theatre for ten years, she is able to use her knowledge of movement and the human body when directing intimate scenes. The combination of these allow her to create intimate moments that complement the story being told, while ensuring the comfortability of everyone involved.

ASSISTANT DIRECTOR | ELLIE ROSE

Ellie is a Welsh theatre director. She trained at the Royal Central School of Speech and Drama and Salford University. Director Credits include; *Broken* (Contact Theatre); *I Am Not A Robot* (Oldham Coliseum Studio); *The Looks Department* (53Two); *Squirrels* (Portsmouth Guildhall); *Meet Me At Dawn* (Hope Mill Theatre); *Tangled & Wildfires* (Vignettes, 22 & 21); *Mortgage* (David Glass Ensemble, AD); *The Well* (Salford Arts Theatre); *When I Grow Up To Be A Man* (The Lowry Studio). She teaches at institutions across the UK and is an associate artist of Created A Monster Theatre.

CASTING DIRECTOR | POLLY JERROLD

Theatre credits include: *Wolves in the road, Paradise Now!* (Bush Theatre); *The Secret Garden, Robin Hood, Antigone, Peter Pan, A Tale of Two Cities, Oliver Twist, To Kill A Mockingbird* tour, *Running Wild* tour (Regent's Park Open Air Theatre); *Chasing Hares, The Secretaries* (Young Vic); *First Touch* (Nottingham Playhouse); *Life of Pi* (Sheffield Theatres, UK Tour & West End); *Waldo's* (Extraordinary Bodies/ Bristol Old Vic); *Rope, Constellations, The Great Gatsby, Pretty Shitty Love, Milky Peaks, Celebrated Virgins, Curtain Up* and *For the Grace of You Go I* (Theatr Clwyd); *Shandyland* (Northern Stage); *One Flew Over the Cuckoo's Nest,*

Tribes (Sheffield Theatres); *Our Lady of Kibeho, Soul, Merlin, Peter and the Starcatcher* (Royal & Derngate); *Two Trains Running* (ETT and Royal & Derngate); *Approaching Empty* (Kiln, Tamasha & Live Theatre); *The Lovely Bones* (Royal & Derngate, Birmingham Rep and Northern Stage); *All's Well That Ends Well* (Shakespeare's Globe); *The Caretaker* (Bristol Old Vic); *The Government Inspector, Tommy, Our Country's Good* (Ramps on the Moon); *The Island Nation* (Arcola); *Brideshead Revisited, A View from the Bridge, Sherlock* (York Theatre Royal); *Anita & Me, Peter Pan, Of Mice and Men, A Christmas Carol, 101 Dalmatians, What Shadows, Folk, Winnie And Wilbur, Back Down, Feed the Beast, I Knew You* (Birmingham Rep); *The Kitchen Sink, Educating Rita* (Hull Truck Theatre); *Sweet Charity, Wit, The Ghost Train* and *Little Shop of Horrors* (Royal Exchange Theatre).

COMPANY STAGE MANAGER | ALEC REECE

Alec studied Drama at Aberystwyth University and has worked in Stage Management for the past fifteen years. He worked at The Lyric Theatre Belfast for two years before freelancing around the UK and abroad. Productions include *Romeo & Juliet* (Royal Exchange Theatre); *Spring and Port Wine, Blonde Bombshells of 1943* (Octagon Theatre, Bolton); *The Syrian Baker* (Farnham Maltings); *Red Ellen* (Northern Stage); *Our Country's Good* (Ramps on the Moon); *Splish Splash* (Oily Cart); *Once* (New Wolsey); *All My Sons* (Rose Theatre Kingston).

Alec has worked on five Rock and Roll pantos at Theatr Clwyd as well as Curtain Up and Truth/Dare.

DEPUTY STAGE MANAGER | TYLA THOMAS

Tyla graduated from the Royal Welsh College of Music and Drama in 2021 with a degree in Stage Management and Technical Theatre. Since leaving university, she has worked on various productions, such as: *Carwyn* (Torch Theatre); *Pijin* (Theatr Genedlaethol Cymru); *Of Mice and Men* (Torch Theatre); *Assassins: The Musical* (WAVDA); *Private Lives* (Torch Theatre) and *Beauty and the Beast* (Torch Theatre).

ASSISTANT STAGE MANAGER | EMMA HARDWICK

Emma graduated from the University of Chester with an English Literature and Creative Writing degree. Work placements include: *Now Is Good* (Storyhouse); *Celebrated Virgins, A Pretty Sh*tty Love* (Theatr Clwyd). Assistant Stage Manager credits: *Sleeping Beauty, Robin Hood, The Great Gatsby* (Theatr Clwyd) and *Black Sabbath – The Ballet* (Birmingham Royal Ballet).

CHARACTERS

In order of appearance

GARETH – late-twenties, estate agent from Pontypridd now based in west Wales.

CARYL – fifties, from west Wales. She, and her husband Meirion, are the only permanent residents of their village.

MAX – mid-thirties, from Bristol, mixed-heritage British/Zambian. He, and his wife Jenny, have just bought the house next door to Caryl and Meirion.

MEIRION – fifties, from west Wales. Caryl's husband.

SEREN – early-thirties, from west Wales now living in Cardiff. Caryl and Meirion's only child.

SETTING

The near future in a house in Porth Y Graith,
a fictional Pembrokeshire coastal village.

AUTHOR'S NOTES

A forward slash (/) marks the point of interruption in overlapping dialogue.

The radio, when on, should only be the weather forecast, white noise, or a mix of the two.

The play follows a traditional three act structure. Each act is defined by its own mood. I have suggested the interval fall within the middle of Act Two, which, whilst not conventional, feels fitting to this play.

PROLOGUE

(Late February. Early morning, still dark.)

*(**GARETH**, dressed smartly and for the cold, carries a branded portfolio folder emblazoned with YOUR WERTH PROPERTIES and a laser distance measurer. He keeps himself busy making various notes until, upon noticing the audience, he gives a warm business-like welcome. With a glint in his eye, he rifles through his folder and then pulls out a prospectus to read from, giving it the big sell.)*

GARETH. Silence. *(Beat.)* To begin at the beginning:[*]

It is spring, *almost*, moonless night in this much sought-after coastal village, starless and bible-black, the cobblestreets silent and the hunched, courters'-and-rabbits' wood limping invisible down to the sloeblack, slow, black, crowblack, farrow-and-ball black, fishingboat-bobbing sea.

And all the people of this lulled prime seaside village, with spectacular panoramic views, are sleeping now.

*(**CARYL** enters wearing wellies, layers of clothing and a bobble hat. She carries a bucket of water in one hand and a cloth in the other. She stops to listen for a moment, growing obviously irritated by what she hears. **GARETH** side-eyes her but, now midstream, does not fully acknowledge her.)*

---

[*] The prologue is adapted from Dylan Thomas' *Under Milk Wood* (1954), which is in the public domain in the United Kingdom.

GARETH. Hush, the babies are sleeping, the farmers, the fishers, the tradesmen and pensioners, cobbler, schoolteacher, postman and publican, the undertaker and the fancy woman, drunkard, dressmaker, preacher, policeman, the webfoot cocklewomen and the tidy / wives.

CARYL. No, they're not love. They all buggered off long ago.

(Blackout.)

ACT ONE

Scene One

(Early morning.)

(Lights up on a kitchen-cum-living area in a Pembrokeshire house.)

(The original house dates to the mid-1800s. The living area at the front of the stage feels traditional, whilst the more modern kitchen area, an extension, probably from the 1980s, is slightly raised at the back of the stage. There is an awkward step in-between the two areas.)

(Upstage, there is a door to the back garden and another to a toilet. Downstage, stairs to upstairs are visible and there is an offstage front door exit. A stone inglenook fireplace dominates one side of the room. There is an old sofa, shelves full of books, photos and an old music system. Fishing and crabbing equipment is spread around the room, with lobster pots piled high upon each other and rods propped up against each other in corners.)

(At the heart of the room is a large dining table. Once this would have been used for family meals and entertaining but now piles

> *of laundry, paperwork and other household items litter the table, leaving just one corner clear enough for two people to eat at. A wall calendar reads February but with very little on it.)*
>
> *(The room is in the middle of a somewhat disorganised but extreme clean and so we find chairs on top of each other, and the furniture pushed at awkward angles, whilst a hoover sits in the middle of the stage.)*
>
> *(**CARYL** is either on her hands and knees, with a dustpan, or up on top of a chair or the table dusting the ceiling. **MAX**, who has just entered via the back door [which remains open], is fresh from the sea wearing a changing robe, a pair of plastic clog shoes and a brightly coloured bobble hat which almost matches **CARYL**'s. He carries a Waitrose tote bag over his shoulder.)*

CARYL. Sut dych chi? *(Slower now.)* Sut dych chi? How / are

MAX. *(He gets it.)* Da iawn, diolch! Da iawn. Sorry, that just sounded a bit erm, a bit *different*. I couldn't quite, on the app, you know, on the app it sounds different.

CARYL. Well, I'm not an app, am I. No, you've caught yourself a live one here Max!

MAX. No, no, it's great. To be able to. IRL. Mae hi'n braf today, *heddiw*, Caryl. Spring has finally sprung in Porth Y Graith. Greeth?

CARYL. Graith. Is February spring? Not in my book. And surely, it's dangerous to be swimming out there this time of year?

> *(**MAX** closes the back door.)*

MAX. God no. It was *sublime. (Pointing at her head.)* Hey, look, we've got matching hats! You're a Pembrokeshire style icon, Caryl.

(**CARYL** *takes her hat off.*)

Is Marion here?

CARYL. Marion?

MAX. Meon?

CARYL. Not quite.

MAX. Sorry.

CARYL. Go on. Have another go.

MAX. Merryman?

CARYL. Mey-ree-on. Meirion.

MAX. Mayran.

CARYL. Oh, I don't know why I'm bothering. He won't care. Nothing ever really upsets Meirion, aside from me that is, *breathing*.

MAX. Right. It's just, well, I'm having to get off shortly.

CARYL. Back *home* is it?

MAX. Well, back to Bristol, yes. The internet connection down here, it's still a bit, you know *(Beat.) patchy*. Hopefully they'll get it sorted soon but I've got to go granular in this meeting with my team end of play.

CARYL. *Granular?* Right. Well, hold on.

(**CARYL** *goes to the bottom of the stairs and shouts up.*)

Meirion! Max, the new one from next door, is here to see you.

MAX. I think I'm in your way. I should wait outside, or I could just pop / back

CARYL. Don't be daft, I'm only having a quick tidy.

> (**CARYL** *lays an old towel on top of a lobster pot.*)

Sit down there whilst you wait. He'll be down in a minute.

> (**MAX** *perches whilst* **CARYL** *tidies around him with exaggerated effort.*)

CARYL. Remind me, what is it you do again Max?

MAX. I'm a consultant. Marketing. Digital mainly.

CARYL. Oh, there we are then, I thought for a minute then that you meant a *proper* consultant. We could do with one of them round here.

MAX. No. Jenny is the one with the proper job.

CARYL. We've not met her yet, have we? Jenny.

MAX. Not yet. *(Beat.)* No, hold on. You did meet her when we first came to view the place?

> (**CARYL** *stares at the ceiling.*)

CARYL. No, I would have remembered. Been a few months since you got the keys to Glyn's place.

MAX. *Our* place. And she's not, *not* coming.

CARYL. Max, be a love and give me a hand will you. See that spider's web up there, I don't think I'll be able to reach it.

> (**MAX** *reaches up or climbs up on a chair to do so.*)

Could you just. No, hold on. Be careful you don't hurt him mind. He has as much right to live here as we do.

MAX. What do you want / me

CARYL. Pass him here. He won't bite.

> (**MAX** *scoops up the spider and gives it to* **CARYL**.*)*

Right then, corryn bach, how about you build a brand-new life for yourself in our shed.

> (**CARYL** *goes out.* **MAX** *realises how wet he is getting the floor and attempts and fails to clean it up.* **CARYL** *re-enters.*)

I hope it's not our wildlife that's keeping Jenny away, is it?

MAX. No, no! She was all set to come down to Graith this time, but something came up.

CARYL. Craith.

MAX. Sorry?

CARYL. Or Y Graith but not Graith. It's incorrect.

MAX. Right.

CARYL. Oh, don't worry, it's those hellish mutations. Enough to make you want to *mutate* yourself, aren't they? Not that, that would be such an awful thing, mind. What would you mutate into? If you could?

MAX. I don't. I've never really thought about / it.

CARYL. I'd be a cont y môr, I would.

MAX. *(Apprehensively.)* Sorry, Caryl, a cont?

CARYL. Y môr. A jellyfish, Max. And then I could just swim away. *Propel* myself away. *(Beat.)* But I'd probably just end up being washed up back on the shore here. Back where I started. Like you on your way now, heading back to England.

> (**MAX** *laughs.*)

MAX. Yeah right. I'm gutted actually. But on the upside, I've just scored myself a cheeky hair appointment back in Bristol, squeezing it in just before this big team call today, so that's a bonus. Don't want them all thinking I've let myself go now I'm WFW.

CARYL. WFW?

MAX. Working From Wales. I have this one particular barber I like, you know, and he's kind of in demand so I / have to.

CARYL. You don't have to explain yourself to me now love. I'd love a new do I would. Just look at the state of my mop, will / you?

MAX. Oh no Caryl, you look great. *(In a Welsh accent.)* Stunning!

CARYL. You need an optician's appointment love not a haircut. *(Beat.)* I used to have a fabulous hairdresser. A Peripatetic she was.

MAX. Oh God! How did that happen? Was it an accident?

CARYL. Peripatetic not parap– a *mobile* hairdresser. Came round here every two months or so to tidy me up she did, and I don't drive see, but she packed it in.

MAX. Did she get a new job?

CARYL. New job? No love. She was living in a place she'd rented for years, and I mean *years*, by the big Tesco in Hav'ford. Anyway, last year, out of the blue, her landlord decides he can make more money letting it out to tourists. And she couldn't find anywhere else so ended up moving in with her sister in Llanelli. So now she's cooped-up in Carmarthenshire, poor bugger, and I'm left looking like Noddy Holder most of the time. *(Beat.)* So, you're off soon, are you?

MAX. Had my final dose of vitamin sea. And now I just need to check the house is all clear before the builders start in a couple of weeks.

CARYL. Builders?

MAX. I had a word with Marion.

CARYL. Meirion.

MAX. Sorry. He's going to keep an eye on them for us.

CARYL. He didn't mention it.

MAX. And so, unless there's some almighty disaster you won't see me, us, until probably May now.

CARYL. Right.

MAX. But you have my number if you need me.

> (**MAX** *walks down to the front of the stage and stares out to sea.*)

Oh God, I'm going to miss that view!

CARYL. You should get a painting done, take it back to Bristol with you.

MAX. That's a great idea. Jenny would love that.

CARYL. You could commission someone local.

MAX. Absolutely. Do you know any local artists?

CARYL. *(Nods.)* Some great ones.

MAX. Really?

CARYL. All gone now.

MAX. Right, yes. *(Beat.)* You mean *Glen* don't you?

CARYL. Glyn. You're living in the house of one of Pembrokeshire's most revered artists! I'm sure they told you he was awarded an MBE for his services to the arts a few years back? Maybe you could pop a blue plaque up, add some value.

> (*The radio turns on by itself. Talk of a storm coming.*)

CARYL. This bloody thing. It's the weather or nothing.

> (**CARYL** *turns it off before attempting to clean some greasy fingerprints off the back window.*)

MAX. It has to be twenty years since they died.

CARYL. Sorry?

MAX. For a plaque. And with it only being two since he, you / know

CARYL. I wasn't even being serious.

MAX. Jenny had a quick look. She's the art fan in our house.

CARYL. Which house? Your Bristol house or Glyn's house? Or do you have another house somewhere? *(Beat.)* I'm joking! And look, I'm sorry I keep calling it Glyn's. I'll get used to it soon enough.

MAX. You know, we actually have a couple of Glen's paintings, that Jenny asked to keep.

CARYL. Oh, right?

MAX. We paid for them. Jenny was keen. I don't really go in / for

CARYL. Which ones?

MAX. There's a one of Ramsey Island and then the other is of some children on top of the erm...

CARYL. Lime Kilns.

MAX. Bingo! Shame he didn't paint one of *this* view.

CARYL. You don't need a painting when you can just open your curtains.

MAX. No, of course. Lucky us.

CARYL. What are you having done?

MAX. Oh, just a trim. Gets out of control surprisingly quickly.

CARYL. I meant to the house.

MAX. Oh, right, LOL! We're just getting new windows put in really, bigger windows to let in some more light and then we're going to extend out a bit at the back, an extra bathroom on the ground floor, well a wet room really with an entrance to outside for when we come off the beach. We're getting an air source heat pump fitted and we'll definitely go solar. Then a new kitchen, with an island and heated floor, all sustainable, side utility, and then bifolds out into the garden.

CARYL. Bifolds?

MAX. Doors. Like the ones in the pink house at the end.

CARYL. Oh, you mean the Thomas's old house? Made a right bugger of that, if you ask me, which of course, no one ever has. Are you keeping Glyn's studio?

MAX. I'm hoping Jenny might fancy it as her office, but it's just got my paddle board in it for now.

CARYL. Well, there we are then.

(**CARYL** *moves away but quickly returns.*)

You know, it used to drive his wife wild, *both* of his wives in fact, just how much time he spent in that studio, but after *she*, the second one, died, well there was no stopping him.

MAX. Was he heartbroken?

CARYL. Sorry?

MAX. I mean do they think that's why, he, you know?

CARYL. No.

MAX. Just strange. Jenny thought.

CARYL. What is?

MAX. Him, just *disappearing* like that.

CARYL. Oh, spooked her has it, love? That's why we've not had the honour of meeting her yet?

MAX. Oh no. No. Jenny's not / really

CARYL. No, no, no, not at all. I can imagine it is a bit *spooky* with you finally being in there now. Old place like that. Full of some *other* person's memories. Someone who just *vanished* one day. Would give me the creeps that. A lot of his stuff still there, is it?

MAX. No not much. A few bits of furniture we bought from his sons.

CARYL. Any more paintings?

MAX. There's some bits and bobs left in the loft, but just old canvases, I think really. Mostly blank, I think. I didn't want to rifle through them too much. Seems a bit weird.

CARYL. You'll just have to take a photo. Show it to Jenny, see if she fancies a visit.

(**MAX**'s *phone rings.*)

MAX. Speak of the devil! Sorry to be rude, but would it be okay if I take this for a minute?

CARYL. Oh no, don't mind me love. You make yourself at home.

MAX. *(To Jenny.)* Jenny, hi!

CARYL. Right. Where the hell is my husband?

MAX. *(To* **CARYL**.*)* There's no rush, honestly.

CARYL. Not for you, maybe.

(**CARYL** *heads upstairs, carrying a basket of laundry with her, calling as she goes.*)

Meirion! / Meirion!

MAX. *(To Jenny.)* I'm just round next door. Dropping off the keys.

> (**MAX** *takes the opportunity to have a look around, perhaps getting his hand stuck in a lobster pot.*)

CARYL. *(From upstairs.)* Meirion! Max is here. Hurry up will you. He needs to speak to / you.

MAX. *(To Jenny.)* Yes that's her now.

CARYL. *(From upstairs.)* Meirion! You're not still asleep, are you?

MAX. *(To Jenny.)* She's eccentric, that's all. You just need to get to know her. Once you meet her, it'll be fine.

CARYL. *(From upstairs.)* He's not here!

MAX. *(To Jenny.)* Right. I knew you had. I said that. Honestly though, I think you'll love her. You just need to play her at her own game. It's kind of fun.

> (**CARYL** *storms downstairs and glares at* **MAX**.)

CARYL. Stay there!

> (**CARYL** *leaves through the front door.* **MAX** *stares out to sea.*)

MAX. *(To Jenny.)* You just need to get down here again Jen. I've never known such peace and quiet.

CARYL. *(Offstage, shouting.)* Meirion!

MAX. *(To Jenny.)* I promise you. We made the right decision. This is for you Jen. For us. A place we can get away from it all and just *relax*.

CARYL. *(Offstage, screaming.)* Meirion!

MAX. *(To Jenny.)* Just what the therapist ordered! Our own little *paradise*.

CARYL. *(Offstage, screaming louder.)* Meirion! Meirion! Oh, for God's sake! Meirion! Max is here for you. Come up here / now.

MAX. *(To Jenny.)* Woah there, I didn't do it by *myself*. I can't believe you just said that.

(**CARYL** *enters.*)

Look, I better go. We'll talk about it later, okay? *(Jenny has already finished the call – he looks at his phone.)* Love you.

CARYL. He was down on the slip fiddling around with his boat. At this time in the morning!

MAX. Amazing that he could hear you from up here. So *peaceful*.

CARYL. Just us again after today.

MAX. Except for our builders.

(**CARYL** *doesn't respond.*)

Sorry Caryl. That was me trying to be funny.

CARYL. Oh right. I didn't get that. Bristol humour, maybe?

MAX. But please do let me know if the builders become a nuisance.

CARYL. Oh, I will. You're not the first to do it mind. But you might just be the last, now that we're the only ones left, well until we finally *depart* anyway.

MAX. *(Shocked.)* No, Caryl!

CARYL. I didn't mean *dead* Max. I just mean if we ever decide to sell up and go.

MAX. You wouldn't, would you?

(**CARYL** *stares at* **MAX** *for a moment, considering her reply.*)

CARYL. You know, I didn't think I'd ever say this. Not out loud anyway. See, Meirion's family built this house in 1863. But this place is all we really have to retire on and it's thanks to your lot that its worth a few bob now.

MAX. Oh / right well.

CARYL. I wasn't actually thanking you! You've got eyes, you can see what's happened to this place. Not really somewhere you'd want to live, *permanently*.

MAX. I don't know. If I *could*, I'd love / to.

CARYL. If you could, you would, but you can't. So, you'll just come down when you can. What a luxury. Things a bit different for us mind. Probably is time for us to go. If I *could* convince Meirion, which seems highly unlikely, but I think maybe, that we could just go somewhere. Not too far. Just somewhere with a bit more life and a few less memories. And a bus service, a doctor and a shop. Not too much to ask for. But, Meirion keeps on saying it wouldn't make sense whilst we're still running the caravan park.

MAX. How long have you had it?

CARYL. The park? We don't own it. We just run it. The current owners are in Dubai. We're the Welsh front see. Actually, they'll probably just stick us in St Fagans when we retire.

(**CARYL** *laughs.* **MAX** *doesn't.*)

MAX. St Fagans? Is that a nursing home?

CARYL. It's a museum. Heritage stuff. It's just outside Cardiff. You could pop in on your way home if you have time.

MAX. Next time, maybe. I wouldn't want Jen to miss out.

(**MEIRION** *enters, wearing working clothes. He is strong but with some stiffness. He carries a toolbox, which he puts down on the floor.*)

CARYL. Finally!

MEIRION. So sorry Max.

(**CARYL** *picks up the toolbox.*)

(*Narked.*) Caryl, don't put those in the shed, I'll need them again in a minute now.

(**CARYL** *drops it.* **MEIRION** *smiles at* **MAX** *attempting to ignore* **CARYL***'s hostility.*)

You didn't say *when* you were coming, and as Caryl had a sudden urge to do an early-morning early-spring clean, I thought I'd better make myself scarce.

MAX. No, no (*Slowly.*) Mae, Mae'n drwg / ddrwg.

CARYL. He's come about his house.

MEIRION. Everything okay at Glan Y Môr, is it?

MAX. I just wanted to drop the keys off, like we / said

CARYL. I meant to ask, Max. Will you be changing that?

MAX. Sorry?

CARYL. The name of Glyn's, sorry, the name of *your* house?

MEIRION. And why would they want to do that then?

CARYL. One of the girls who owns *Swn Y Môr* with her sisters told me they were thinking about turning their place into *The Nightjar's Rest (Snorts with laughter.)* when did you ever see a nightjar round here then?

MAX. Well, we won't be changing *Glan Y Môr*, Caryl. That's why we're here after all, to be beside the sea.

CARYL. Not Jenny though. She's in Bristol.

MEIRION. Well, it's lovely to have you here, isn't it Caryl? And we'll have to grab a pint together when they open The Ship again.

MAX. Is it really closed *all* winter now?

MEIRION. Bastards at the Brewery decided that was a smart idea a few years back.

MAX. You know, I hadn't really clocked that when we bought the place! Proper schoolboy error.

CARYL. Lucky they can't take that view away then, isn't it Max. Only thing stopping us from blowing our brains out this time of year.

MEIRION. She's joking.

(**CARYL** *gives a false smile.*)

CARYL. Meirion, is it you that has been putting mucky fingers all over these windows? It's been a right bugger to get off.

MEIRION. Why would I have done that?

CARYL. As soon as I clean them off, they're back again. Someone is playing funny buggers with me. And look all this dirt by the back door? Where the hell has that all come from?

MEIRION. Can I ask, what is this sudden clean in honour of? We don't have people coming over do we?

CARYL. Have we heck! Just thought I'd cheer myself up.

MAX. Oh, I love a good clean.

CARYL. I don't. I hate it.

MEIRION. *(It clicks.)* You haven't have you?

CARYL. Well, it's no skin off your nose is it. Not really.

MEIRION. What have you done that for? I *specifically* asked you not do that. Are you trying to drive me *(Stops, remembering* **MAX** *is there.)* So sorry Max. You wanted to leave your keys with me.

MAX. No, no, it's fine. Honestly. Jenny and I. We've been known to have the occasional *misunderstanding*. Like our juju is just not aligning you know. But that's to be expected, right, after so long. Anyway, yes, if you don't mind keeping an eye on the old place and I got you this. For both of you. *(He pulls out a bottle of whiskey and some keys from his bag.)* To say thank you. I really do appreciate it. And here's the keys.

MEIRION. Well, that's very kind of you Max. Looks like a very nice drop. Did, er, did Glyn's sons pick up those bits left in the loft, that you were worried about?

MAX. No. I texted his son, *Owen*, is it? But I never heard back. I think I'll tell the builders just to dump it all once they start. Anyway, any issues, just text or call. Whatever.

*(**CARYL** opens the back door for **MAX**.)*

MEIRION. We will.

MAX. Right, the M4 awaits! I can't wait to get back up here in the summer. A drink at The Ship and I was wondering, maybe you could take me out on the boat? I'd love to get some fishing tips from an old pro like you.

> *(**CARYL** grows tired of waiting for **MAX** to leave and she turns the hoover on and starts to clean, so that **MAX** and **MEIRION** must raise their voices to be heard.)*

MEIRION. Happy to. Before life at the site gets too busy, mind. Get you some fresh crabs rather than those you had out of our freezer last week.

MAX. Ace. Diolch! Well, I better skedaddle, you two take good care of yourselves. Hwyl fawr.

MEIRION. Hwyl Fawr. Mind how you go.

CARYL. Hwyl. Love to Jenny!

> (**MAX** *leaves.* **CARYL** *turns the hoover off.* **MEIRION** *stares at her.)*

MEIRION. So, what time are they coming?

CARYL. Two p.m. So, you can piss off out if you're not interested.

> *(Blackout.)*

Scene Two

(Later that day.)

(The room is slightly more presentable, mostly due to CARYL's efforts in the first scene.)

(GARETH stands centre stage, with CARYL looking on. MEIRION sits at his laptop, pretending to ignore them both.)

GARETH. *(With real enthusiasm.)* I love this! Deceptively spacious. *(Looking out through the back window.)* And there's room to extend if a buyer wanted to?

CARYL. Absolutely. Plenty of garden out the back. *(Side-eyes MEIRION.)* Real sun trap in the morning just by here, well it was until my husband built that ridiculous shed.

GARETH. Storage is always a bonus!

CARYL. Of course. You're absolutely right. But not to me, as he never actually uses the bugger. Have you seen our view?

(They both stare out towards the audience.)

GARETH. Yes, it's very nice Mrs Hughes

CARYL. Very nice? It's *spectacular*.

GARETH. I can see why you've stayed here so long.

CARYL. Well at least the view doesn't get old, whereas I'm afraid the house is far from *postcard perfection*.

GARETH. Oh, don't worry about that, many buyers like a blank canvas.

CARYL. Right. Keen to put their own mark on the place?

GARETH. Just like you did.

CARYL. I suppose we tried. My husband built this extension himself, but this house has always been in his family, and whilst it is not without its issues, we've never had the urge to completely wipe away someone else's existence. Oh, watch yourself.

> *(Too late, he trips on the step, but manages to stable himself.)*

I am so sorry. Are you okay love? As I say not without its issues.

GARETH. No harm done. These old properties are full of such character.

CARYL. But that's the new bit that he built. This door here, buggered too. Doesn't close properly anymore. See, I don't think it really works, this extension. This *kitchen*. Do you?

GARETH. I think this house embodies the essence of Porth Y Graith. You could absolutely find the right buyer for it.

CARYL. You would say that.

GARETH. I'm certain of it.

CARYL. No. That's your job to say that. What I need is an *honest* opinion please.

> *(Pause.)*

GARETH. Well, I think this kitchen probably could, perhaps, have been built in a more sympathetic style to the rest of the property but that's not / to say

CARYL. Exactly! I've tried to make it blend in more with the rest of the house, but you know "you can't make a silk purse out of a sow's ear".

GARETH. Sorry?

CARYL. It means you can't improve the unimprovable: "put lipstick on a pig and it's still a pig".

GARETH. Oh, so like, "you can't polish a turd"?

(**CARYL** *absorbs this.*)

CARYL. Exactly like that, yes.

GARETH. Can I make an observation?

CARYL. Go on.

GARETH. Well, it's strange.

CARYL. What is?

GARETH. Well, most people who invite me to value their property wouldn't necessarily talk about their homes, in the way you do.

CARYL. And?

GARETH. Well, with you, well it's almost like. Well, it's almost like you don't actually want to sell it.

MEIRION. No *almost* about it.

CARYL. Ignore him please.

MEIRION. I think this is her idea of fun. A little game of make-believe.

CARYL. Don't be so ridiculous.

MEIRION. To cheer herself up. She's a fantasist. Or maybe she just fancied the company. We're not going anywhere. Ever. I didn't even know you were coming round today.

CARYL. Rubbish. I told you I'd called them up.

MEIRION. And I told you to bugger off. I'm sorry but she's giving you the run-around.

GARETH. It's fine. Honestly. People are often uneasy about this process. But I am more than happy to take things at a speed you *both* feel comfortable with.

CARYL. Can we at least let Mr Phillips.

GARETH. Gareth, please.

CARYL. Can we at least let *Gareth* do the valuation? Just to know what we're sitting on. We're not getting any younger Meirion. Can he at least do that? Humour me?

GARETH. I'd be very happy to oblige.

MEIRION. I'm sure you would. A house like this, in a *location* like this. Worth every effort trying to convince us to go.

CARYL. As the boy is here, let him do his job.

>   *(Pause. **MEIRION** doesn't say anything.)*

Well, go on then love.

GARETH. *(Apprehensively.)* You sure?

>   *(**CARYL** nods enthusiastically. **GARETH** looks to **MEIRION**.)*

MEIRION. Well, as long as you know you'll be wasting your time. / Don't think

CARYL. See, I knew he'd want to know. Pretending like he wasn't interested.

GARETH. Okay, so. *(Composes himself.)* I'm pleased to say that the demand for homes has been growing steadily for many years. Do you have any thoughts who you might, *theoretically speaking*, be looking to sell to?

CARYL. Sorry?

GARETH. Well, given the significant interest in the area, many of the people I've looked after have had certain *stipulations* in terms of potential buyers, you know.

CARYL. How do you mean?

GARETH. Well, some people are wanting buyers with some links to the area, or they have to be Welsh, or no short term lets or second homes. That sort of thing.

CARYL. Now there's funny.

GARETH. Whilst there may be certain ambitions at the start of the process, people do tend to end up taking the highest price offered. And I have a lot of people from places like Cheltenham, Bristol, Bath on my books looking for a seaside bolthole, especially now that people aren't expected to be in the office every day.

CARYL. We've got our fill of Saes here.

GARETH. I understand your hesitation. But they do have the capital available and are eager to extend their portfolios. Nothing wrong with that. However, I have strong links in Cardiff if you'd be more comfortable with / that?

CARYL. Cardiff? The couple from Penarth up in Coed Môr, Meirion knew his Tadcu, Meibion Glyndwr he was. What he'd think of his grandson living the life of riley in Cardiff, a lawyer and loaded it looks like, and then up here whenever the city gets a bit too sweaty for him and his stuck-up wife. I've probably got more in common with the new ones next door, not that we've actually met *her* yet.

GARETH. The lovely couple from Bristol? How are they settling in?

CARYL. Oh! Sold to them, did you?

GARETH. Max, isn't it? Top bloke. Smashing client. So honest and straightforward.

*(**CARYL** grows increasingly frustrated.)*

CARYL. You do realise that apart from us, that house belonged to the last real resident of this village?

GARETH. Look, I can see you obviously have strong feelings / about

CARYL. Strong feelings? *You* moved in some couple from England, who know nothing about this / place.

*(**MEIRION** starts laughing.)*

MEIRION. Oh, you're in for it now butt. This must be why she asked you over. No one else left here to listen to her moan.

CARYL. Well, *you* certainly don't.

GARETH. They seem very nice. Eager to fit in.

CARYL. But they have no connection to the place, no real reason to be here apart from the fact he likes to freeze his nuts off in the sea in winter.

GARETH. I realise this is an emotional subject for you. But I simply took instruction from his sons.

CARYL. But what happens if Glyn comes back here tomorrow and finds some bloke from Bristol's paddleboard in his studio? He won't like that I can tell you.

GARETH. Well, that would be. Awful. Truly, awful. But perhaps quite impossible?

CARYL. Not impossible. You want to watch out.

GARETH. Oh, I've heard *all* about his *artistic temperament*, but I'm not overly concerned for my safety given that he's now *dead*.

CARYL. Not *dead*.

MEIRION. Stop it now / Caryl.

CARYL. *Presumed* dead. He still could come back. He must have been totally twp to put it in his son's names.

MEIRION. Stop going on about that man will you. He's not coming back.

CARYL. You don't know that for sure. No one does.

(They all stare awkwardly at each other for a moment.)

GARETH. It's a very personal thing, one's own house. Not just bricks and mortar, are they? I really do understand that. I do. But from my experience, they can mean very different things to different people.

CARYL. *(Making a money hand gesture.)* And we all know what they mean to you.

GARETH. Can I ask if you would actually like me to value your property today or if you might / prefer

CARYL. I'm assuming we'd just be looking at something not far off what Glyn's place went for.

GARETH. Well, yes and no.

MEIRION. Yes and no?

GARETH. Things have changed a bit recently.

*(**GARETH** moves around the room, looking around, suddenly more apprehensive.)*

This property really is full of such fantastic potential.

MEIRION. In what way have things changed?

GARETH. Senedd?

MEIRION. What?

GARETH. The Welsh Government.

MEIRION. I know what Senedd means. What about it?

GARETH. Well, see, there's a potential change afoot, which may have an impact on our conversations. I actually wondered, when Mrs Hughes called me, if maybe you knew already, which is why you'd asked me over? No?

CARYL. I have no idea what you're talking about.

GARETH. Right, okay. Well, okay, I don't want to worry you but it's a sort of Second Home Strategy, some are calling it. I'm told they're debating it all at the moment.

MEIRION. Debates do bugger all. It's action we need.

GARETH. Actually, it seems to have had some serious traction this time.

CARYL. Hallelujah.

GARETH. Looks like there's going to be some new legislation coming in.

MEIRION. And that is?

GARETH. It's not entirely clear yet but more than likely, what's been mooted and as I say, seems to be getting some real support, is a sort of *cap* on the number of second homes and holiday lets. And that *cap* would apply *here*. To this village. To your home.

MEIRION. Which means what exactly?

CARYL. He's saying that we're not going to be able to sell this house. To anyone. Ever.

GARETH. No! No, I'm not saying that. What I'm saying is that there is a *possibility* that you may only be able to sell to someone who doesn't own a *primary* residence elsewhere.

CARYL. Right. And can I ask, in your professional opinion, who would want to actually live here all by themselves? Totally isolated for most of the year. Cut off. Abandoned. Everything else and everyone else gone. Forgotten. And, even if you could find that unique individual, not in need or want of human interaction or basic services even, they're certainly not going to pay over the odds for the privilege now, are they?

GARETH. Quite. But it's not a done deal, nor, more importantly, is it widely known about yet, so if we were to move at some speed, and price to sell, it might not be as bad as you think. Just in the nick of time, so to speak. *(Beat.)* So, shall we carry on then? Is the view just as *spectacular* from upstairs? Or maybe I could take a quick look in the garden?

(Silence.)

No. Right, well, I think I better leave you two to discuss it all. Look, I am sorry if I've caught you off guard. But, to put it bluntly, if you want to *maximise* the value of your property then *now* really is the time to sell. Here's my card.

*(**GARETH** leaves it on the side. He goes to leave but returns.)*

I doubt you remember me, but my uncle used to live in the village. I was down here every summer.

CARYL. We get a lot of *tourists*.

GARETH. Yes, of course. Right, okay. Bye then. Have a lovely weekend.

*(**GARETH** exits. **CARYL** puts her shoes on.)*

MEIRION. He's pulling our legs. Winding us up. It'll be nothing. No need to go anywhere.

CARYL. And you'd love that wouldn't you! I'm going to the site. Maes y Coed called. Their sheep got into the glamping field again. I'll be back by tea.

*(**CARYL** exits)*

(Blackout.)

Scene Three

(That evening.)

*(**CARYL** is sat at the table, attempting to finish her food. **MEIRION** is in the downstairs toilet.)*

MEIRION. *(Sudden shouting from the toilet.)* It just doesn't make any sense!

CARYL. What?

MEIRION. *You!* You don't make any sense. I don't understand, how can you just change your bloody tune like that, after all these years?

CARYL. Meirion, we just agreed not to talk about this anymore.

*(The toilet flushes and **MEIRION** enters.)*

MEIRION. But you always said they'd have to carry you out of here in a coffin.

CARYL. There's still time for that. And I've not said that for years. Years! Did you not wash your hands?

MEIRION. I'm about to do the dishes. We won't finish work for another fifteen, maybe even twenty years. And it's not like we're going to get jobs anywhere else.

CARYL. Rubbish.

MEIRION. Not at our age.

CARYL. I feel like I'm repeating myself here, but you don't seem to be able to grasp the graveness of this situation. We are not ever, *ever*, going to be able to save as much as we'd lose in the value of this place. And apart from this place we have nothing else to retire on. This is all we've / got.

MEIRION. So, after all these years of fighting our corner, we're just going to give up?

CARYL. Look at this place. We lost the fight a long time ago. If we sell now, we get a chance for a new start. Away from here. If we don't sell, we're stuck here, and we'll be utterly, utterly skint and more miserable than we are now.

(**MEIRION** *heads back to the toilet.*)

Where are you going now?

MEIRION. I don't think I'd finished.

(**MEIRION** *goes into the toilet.*)

(**CARYL** *now alone looks around the room, feeling very alone. Suddenly the radio turns on by itself and the back door blows open. Soil softly blowing in from outside.* **CARYL** *turns it off and shuts the door.*)

CARYL. This place.

(**MEIRION** *re-enters.*)

MEIRION. False alarm.

CARYL. Time we pack up and go whilst we still can.

MEIRION. But this is *our* home. Our daughter was born here. *I* was born here. My great-great-grandfather and everyone in-between was born here.

CARYL. They wouldn't recognise it.

MEIRION. That's not a reason to go. To give up.

CARYL. This place would halve in value, mark my words. We can't afford to lose that sort of money Meirion. We're not exactly flush. If we don't act fast, we'll be ruined.

MEIRION. We do okay.

CARYL. Oh my God! Is that a joke?

MEIRION. Everyone's feeling the pinch.

CARYL. You wouldn't think it if you looked round here. This village has never looked so good.

MEIRION. Exactly.

CARYL. But none of that adds up. It doesn't add up. We're not the *same* as them. For *them*, money makes money. But not for us, because we never had any to start with.

MEIRION. But the site is doing well. No worries about our jobs.

CARYL. They'll get rid of us soon enough. And what happens then?

MEIRION. No point worrying about that now though, love. It's a long way off.

CARYL. Am I going mad, here? We've been banking on what this house is worth. We always knew we'd need to sell at some point.

MEIRION. Did we hell. Not everything boils down to money. If we just go, then that really is it for this village.

CARYL. Stop burying your head in the sand. We've bugger all savings and bugger all pensions. We've made a right mess of it. You know that.

MEIRION. Do you not think it's our *duty* to stay?

CARYL. I don't think duty comes into it anymore.

(**MEIRION** *laughs.*)

MEIRION. *Duty* is your middle name!

CARYL. And what good has that done me?

MEIRION. What about our jobs?

(**CARYL** *cries out in despair.*)

CARYL. We're going round in circles here. We can't count on them keeping us on. They've no loyalty to us. And we'll get new jobs.

MEIRION. Not at our age.

CARYL. *At our age?* Okay then, well, at our age, do you not think we need to be thinking about being closer to a hospital perhaps? How long did I have to wait for that ambulance the year before last? I could have very easily died!

MEIRION. It was only gallstones. Bloody drama queen!

CARYL. We didn't know that at the time. You thought I was a goner! And we'll get work somewhere else, even if it's just seasonal but that won't matter because we'll have the lump sum from this place.

MEIRION. But this is our *home* Caryl!

CARYL. Really Meirion? Where the *heart* is? You can hardly bring yourself to look at me these days.

> *(Knock at the door. They are both startled.* **CARYL** *looks at her watch.* **MEIRION** *gets up and goes to the door.)*

MEIRION. Well, I never! Hello stranger.

CARYL. Who is it?

MEIRION. Hold on.

> *(**MEIRION** opens the door.)*

CARYL. *(Panicked.)* Who the hell is it?

MEIRION. Look who's here.

> *(Their daughter,* **SEREN***, walks in. She's wearing an oversized coat and carrying a bag of Christmas presents and an overnight bag.)*

SEREN. Hello you two.

CARYL. Seren!

MEIRION. I didn't hear a car.

SEREN. I left it by the old post office and walked up. Wanted to surprise you both. You okay mam?

CARYL. Frightened the life out of me.

SEREN. It's so good to see you.

MEIRION. Come here.

> (**MEIRION** *moves towards* **SEREN** *but she nervously backs away.*)

Is everything okay?

SEREN. Yeah. Everything is great. Really, really great.

MEIRION. So, come here and give your old dad a cwtch then.

SEREN. I just. I need to. Hold on. Right. Okay. Let me just.

> (**SEREN** *takes a deep breath.*)

Are you ready for *another* surprise?

> (**SEREN** *puts two Christmas gift bags on the table,* **MEIRION** *looks round for their Christmas gift to* **SEREN***, which was tidied away in the first scene.*)

MEIRION. Now where did we put *your* present. Your mam's been on a cleaning rampage today.

SEREN. I'm not talking about these.

> (**SEREN** *takes off her coat to reveal that she is very obviously pregnant.*)

I'm talking about *this*.

CARYL. Oh my God.

MEIRION. Seren! Look at you.

CARYL. What the hell?

MEIRION. Well, I never.

CARYL. I don't know what to.

> *(Stunned silence.)*

Is that real?

SEREN. Yes, of course.

> *(**CARYL** and **MEIRION** stare at their daughter, speechless.)*

Is that all you're going to say?

MEIRION. Congratulations! Marvellous news. You look incredible Seren.

> *(**MEIRION** hugs **SEREN**.)*

SEREN. Diolch *dad*.

MEIRION. Really wonderful. Isn't it Caryl?

CARYL. Is it? A bit of a shock. I didn't. Did we know? I don't think I knew that you were. I didn't know that you were with anyone. So, you've finally met someone, have you?

SEREN. Not really.

CARYL. Not really?

SEREN. No. Not really. Can I just use the loo?

MEIRION. Of course. You know where it is. And I'll stick the kettle on.

CARYL. Not really? What does that mean?

MEIRION. Give Seren a chance to explain.

SEREN. Can I just use the toilet please.

CARYL. I just. I don't understand what that means.

SEREN. I'm literally about to wet myself.

(**SEREN** *heads to the downstairs toilet.*)

CARYL. Hold on, your dad's just been in there, I hope it's alright.

SEREN. Mam!

CARYL. Let me just check.

(**CARYL** *pops in and out of the toilet in a flash.*)

Looks fine! I'll get you a fresh towel.

SEREN. It's only me!

CARYL. I know and look at you. How far along are you Seren?

SEREN. Oh, you know. A few months. Just over halfway I suppose. Coming up to five months now, I guess.

CARYL. *(Taken aback.)* Five months!

(**SEREN** *moves round* **CARYL** *to get to the toilet.*)

SEREN. Mam, seriously now, I'm desperate!

CARYL. You could have called.

SEREN. *(On her way into the toilet.)* I wanted to tell you in person rather than over the phone.

(**SEREN** *finally closes the toilet door.*)

CARYL. What the bloody hell is going on?

MEIRION. How would I know?

CARYL. Because I know she talks to you and not me. And all the time she's been hiding this.

MEIRION. Tread carefully now okay. She looks very happy.

CARYL. I never thought she'd have a one-night stand, did you?

MEIRION. We don't know that's what's happened.

CARYL. Seren might be your little angel, but I very much doubt it was an immaculate conception.

MEIRION. Caryl!

CARYL. I know it's been a long time, but I expect you can just about remember how it all works. She's never even seemed that interested in being in a relationship. And anytime I've tried to talk to her about it, she just shuts me down.

MEIRION. Just give her a chance to explain.

CARYL. She gets that from you.

(Toilet flushes.)

And she's already five months along. Is she trying to give me a heart attack?

MEIRION. Let her explain.

CARYL. Now we know why she didn't show up at all over Christmas. She can normally just about stand to visit us for twenty-four hours but not even that this year.

*(**SEREN** comes back in.)*

MEIRION. Your mam was just saying that we missed not having you here at Christmas.

SEREN. I know, I am sorry. I wanted to come / but

MEIRION. Don't worry about that now. Sit down love.

SEREN. Oh no dad, I'm fine.

CARYL. Your dad's right, you should sit down.

SEREN. I said I'm fine mam. Honestly. How's your hip dad?

MEIRION. Bit of a bugger. Old before my time. This cold weather doesn't help.

SEREN. That's why I got you these.

> (**SEREN** *passes them a gift bag each.* **MEIRION** *pulls out a heated seat pad from his bag.* **CARYL** *puts her bag on the table, without looking in it.* **MEIRION** *reads from the box.*)

MEIRION. *Ground-breaking heat technology.*

SEREN. You sit on them. One for you too mam. Don't want you two oldies dying of cold now do we? And these are more economical than having the heating on all the time.

CARYL. We don't have the heating on all the time. And sorry, love, the last thing I want to do is upset you, but do you think you could tell me who the, who it is that you're having this baby with?

SEREN. Would you like to look at his profile?

CARYL. On Facebook?

SEREN. No. His donor profile, mam.

CARYL. Donor?

SEREN. Yes.

> (*Silence.*)

CARYL. You don't mean *sperm* donor?

SEREN. No! I mean, *yes*, I do mean that.

CARYL. You're having a baby with a sperm donor?

SEREN. No, I'm having a baby by myself. I used a sperm donor to conceive. His part started and ended there.

CARYL. Right.

MEIRION. Well, you look very well, Seren. Doesn't she Caryl?

CARYL. Right.

MEIRION. Positively glowing!

CARYL. Does anyone mind if I have a drink? Meirion, where is that bottle that Max gave you?

SEREN. Max?

MEIRION. Our new neighbour.

> (**CARYL** *finds the bottle and pours herself a glass of whiskey.*)

SEREN. Next door? How did his sons get rid of it so quickly? It's only been, what, two years?

MEIRION. It was in their names. Glyn did it years ago when he married his *second* wife apparently.

SEREN. *They* probably pushed him off that cliff then, get their hands on it and make a fortune. This Max must be loaded. Where's he from?

MEIRION. Bristol.

SEREN. Is he?

CARYL. Never mind that now Seren. *(Pointing at **SEREN**'s belly.)* Back to the *elephant* in the room.

MEIRION. Your mam is just a bit taken aback by this love.

CARYL. The understatement of the year. I don't even know where to start.

SEREN. Then perhaps don't. Why don't you let that sink in and we can talk about it tomorrow. I'm happy to walk you through the whole process and you can ask me as many questions as you like but what I don't want is you getting all upset and angry at me and saying something you'll regret.

CARYL. How dare you walk in here, after God knows how long, acting like this is all totally normal.

SEREN. It's more common than you might expect.

CARYL. What did we do wrong, Meirion? Was I that awful a mam?

MEIRION. Caryl!

SEREN. Mam!

CARYL. Well, I must have been, for you to feel that you couldn't talk to me about it.

SEREN. You're making it super easy now, that's for sure.

CARYL. Explain it to me then. Don't treat me like I'm stupid, just because I'm old.

SEREN. You're not old, mam.

CARYL. No! And neither are you! You're only thirty-two.

SEREN. I've spent years being told I should chase some dream that just wasn't ever going to come true. Not for me anyway. Years being told that eventually I'd meet someone. That someone would choose me. Well, instead, *I* chose me.

CARYL. How beautiful. Rehearsed that did you? And what about this baby? What *choice* do they get? They just have to grow up without a dad?

SEREN. Oh mam! Not everyone can have the perfect upbringing like you had.

CARYL. That's what you think is it?

SEREN. How many unwanted children are born in this world? Children who grow up without their parents' love. Whereas *this* child will know they were wanted so much that I was willing to do it all alone.

CARYL. But look at you and your dad. How close you are. He'd do anything for you. Anything. Didn't you want to give them that? I just wished you'd talked to us about this. Thought it all through a bit more.

SEREN. I wasn't going to gamble away the prospect of becoming a mam.

CARYL. But to deny a child a father, Seren. That's just. It's. I can't help but feel that's just not fair on them.

SEREN. So, would you have preferred I had a child with any old Tom, Dick or Harry? No way. I wouldn't do that to her.

CARYL. To *her*? It's a girl?

(**SEREN** *nods.*)

MEIRION. Bloody hell.

(**CARYL** *chokes up. She turns away to compose herself.*)

Caryl.

CARYL. I'm alright.

SEREN. Sorry mam, if / I've

CARYL. Just give me a minute.

SEREN. Are you okay, mam?

CARYL. I'm just. I just wasn't expecting this you know. And now, you're here. Like this.

SEREN. And I'm *here* because I want you two to be a huge part of this little girl's life.

MEIRION. No other grandparents to share her with!

CARYL. That's a bonus I suppose.

SEREN. *(Teasing.)* See. I knew you'd come round in the end.

(**CARYL** *stares at* **SEREN** *for a moment.*)

CARYL. Are you sure that's real? You're not pulling my leg are you?

SEREN. Here's the donor's profile, look at that if you need convincing.

(**SEREN** *passes* **CARYL** *her phone.*)

CARYL. He's from Norway!

SEREN. You get more details about them from there than you do here. Really top-class specimens, screened for absolutely everything. And if you get it from Norway, you get to see a photo of them as a toddler, look. In the UK, you just get a pen portrait. And a portrait rather than a photo, I mean, they're not the same, are they? A portrait is open to a level of interpretation, of a person. A photo is hard facts.

CARYL. So, you had to go over there for the treatment?

SEREN. No, they shipped it to Cardiff.

CARYL. Bloody Vikings!

MEIRION. Does he have the right to? Can he get involved?

SEREN. That can't happen. He's open to being contacted once she reaches adulthood but he already has his own children. This is something totally separate to that.

CARYL. But why would he do it?

SEREN. Kindness, I think. A sense of humanity.

CARYL. Or maybe he just wants his sperm to invade foreign soil?

SEREN. Whatever. I really don't care. I just have my baby now. That's all that matters. Another one of us. Our family.

MEIRION. You can take her foraging for bilberries like you did with Seren.

CARYL. I had to drag her up that mountain.

SEREN. Oh, come on, I wasn't that bad and it's not a mountain. Beachcombing on the foreshore then? I always loved that.

CARYL. If we're still here.

SEREN. *(Amused.)* Oh right! Been binging on *A Place in the Sun* again have you mam?

MEIRION. Leave it now, Caryl.

CARYL. She needs to know the situation.

SEREN. Know what?

MEIRION. Seren really doesn't need to be worrying about this now, does she? Not in her condition.

SEREN. I'm pregnant. I'm not dying.

CARYL. There's an issue.

SEREN. Your gallbladder again?

CARYL. No, with the Government. Looks like they have finally decided to do something about the fact they've turned this place into a ghost-town, well ghost-village.

SEREN. Well, that's great, isn't it?

CARYL. No, not so great.

SEREN. I don't follow.

CARYL. From what we can find online, it's being suggested that in any area which has under fifty percent of houses as primary residences, you will no longer be able to sell to someone wanting to purchase a house as a second home or holiday let.

MEIRION. As if that will actually happen.

SEREN. Am I being thick? That's what you've always wanted, isn't it?

MEIRION. It would have been great fifty, even ten, years ago. Too late / now.

CARYL. If that law gets passed the value of this place plummets and we have nothing left to retire on. Or leave to you.

SEREN. I don't need anything. I don't want anything. Not if it means you selling this place. This has been in our family for generations.

MEIRION. Exactly!

CARYL. Yes, we're well aware of that.

SEREN. Mam, you can't do this to Dad. It's not fair.

CARYL. Why am I getting the blame?

SEREN. When is this happening?

MEIRION. It's not.

CARYL. Could be six months from now. Maybe less.

SEREN. I cannot believe you're even considering it!

CARYL. It might be the only option, Seren.

SEREN. But you've stayed here for years, regardless of it all. Regardless of. Regardless of anything. Why the hell would you suddenly want to go now?

MEIRION. *(Ignored.)* I think we should / probably.

CARYL. Maybe you've been gone too long to understand.

MEIRION. Caryl.

SEREN. Oh, this, again! I promised myself I wouldn't let you do this today. But you're punishing me again. Aren't you?

CARYL. For what?

SEREN. For going!

CARYL. Don't be so ridiculous.

SEREN. This is what you always do.

CARYL. This is what *you* always do, more like.

SEREN. What does that mean?

MEIRION. *(Ignored again.)* Will you both / just.

CARYL. Acting like you're the victim.

SEREN. You're a fine one to talk!

CARYL. Okay then, just out of interest, where exactly would you put the hot tub once you finally get your hands on the place?

SEREN. What?

CARYL. Seems to be essential now. That and a wood burner. Rustic. People love that. Three nights minimum.

SEREN. That's not fair mam. You have no idea.

CARYL. So, you would actually *want* to live here, would you?

SEREN. It's not that simple.

CARYL. No. I thought not. You don't want to live here. In fact, you can hardly bring yourself to visit us here. But you want us to *stay* here. All alone. Cut off. Not needed by anyone apart from a few months a year when the holiday makers rock up looking for someone to moan at.

SEREN. This place is Dad's roots, and I know I'm not here all the time but it's *my* roots too, you can't do this mam.

CARYL. Roots! Don't you dare talk to me about roots. It's very clear that's not top of your priority list Seren. Especially when it comes to having a baby!

SEREN. Right. You know, actually, it might do you good to move away from here, give you a chance to live in the real world.

CARYL. So, we're agreed then?

SEREN. Fine. Go. This isn't the village I grew up in anyway. I couldn't live here even if I wanted it to.

CARYL. If you wanted to? Well, we all know you just do what you want, when you want, regardless of the consequences. No matter if it makes other people miserable. No matter if it means a baby being born without a father.

SEREN. Well, coming from someone who so obviously thrives off being miserable, you should be bloody well thanking me!

(Blackout.)

Scene Four

(The next morning.)

*(**MEIRION** is fixing a lobster pot. **CARYL** stands at the back door staring down at the floor in front of her.)*

CARYL. It's back.

MEIRION. What is?

CARYL. All this soil again.

(She peers under the door.)

Is it blowing in do you think?

MEIRION. *(Ignoring her.)* I'll have a look in a minute now.

CARYL. *(Pointing at the window.)* And these fingerprints. They're oily it feels like. I'll have to try something stronger on them. Where's that turps?

MEIRION. What turps?

CARYL. I can smell it.

MEIRION. I've not been using any turps. I don't think we even have turps in the house.

CARYL. I'll try some Fairy instead. Is she still not up?

MEIRION. No, not yet. She obviously needs the sleep. I did have a peep at her but she's out for the count. Looks like she did as a little girl.

CARYL. Not so little now!

MEIRION. I know this is a surprise for you, but / do you not

CARYL. A surprise?

MEIRION. It's going to take time for you. For us both to adjust to this. But if it makes Seren happy, then I'm happy. And I'd appreciate it if you two could *try* to get along.

CARYL. We all said things we shouldn't have.

MEIRION. I didn't.

CARYL. Tell me Meirion, where do you feel the loneliest? Here in *this* village or up there on that pedestal of yours?

MEIRION. *(Ignoring her.)* Seren has never been one for convention. I thought you liked that about her?

CARYL. But to do it all by herself?

(**CARYL** *looks at the heated seat pad that* **SEREN** *gave her, plugs it in and sits on it.*)

MEIRION. She'll be fine. You hardly needed me.

CARYL. That's not true.

MEIRION. How long were you upstairs in that bedroom with her? Just the two of you? The pair of you in our bed. Me in the spare room.

CARYL. She was a hungry little bugger.

MEIRION. Like a little fishing boat bobbing up and down on your chest. And nobody else could get a look in. My mam almost went cwcw waiting to get a proper cwtch. But you didn't care. You knew what was best for her. And she'll know what's best for her little girl.

CARYL. But when she went off to college, you were beside yourself. It was like I didn't exist anymore. Once she'd gone, something changed in you.

MEIRION. She was only sixteen. Felt too soon. And maybe I knew she'd never come back. Not really.

CARYL. You'd do anything for her. I know you would. If anyone hurt her. God help them. I can't imagine what you'd do. You love her more than anything. But she's taking all that away from that child. And I'm sorry, but I can't bear it!

(A noise from upstairs.)

MEIRION. She's up. Leave it now.

*(As **SEREN** comes downstairs they switch to a sunnier tone.)*

MEIRION. Morning love.

SEREN. Bore da.

*(**CARYL** shifts about in her seat.)*

CARYL. Bore da, love. It's hot this thing!

SEREN. I think that's the point, mam.

CARYL. Seren, what we talked about last / night.

SEREN. I don't want another row.

CARYL. I was just tired and got a bit worked up love, is all. You know me. Sit down, I'll make you some breakfast.

SEREN. Not just yet. I'm a little bit *(Pulls a queasy expression.)*. I think I'll go for a walk first.

CARYL. Quick cup then?

*(**CARYL** goes to make her a cup of tea, whilst **MEIRION** and **SEREN** walk downstage together to look out to sea where **CARYL** can't hear their conversation.)*

MEIRION. Do you know how lovely it is having you here? I could burst. I wish you'd come home more often. We've not done something to make you feel that you can't / come.

SEREN. No dad. No, of course not. But I will just say, if you did think you should / move

MEIRION. Please love, don't worry about that now.

SEREN. But if it came to it, then of course that's your decision. And you're right, it's not like I'm down here much anymore but I was hoping, now with, well things have changed, I was planning to be down here a bit more you know.

MEIRION. You're always welcome here Seren. This is your home.

> (**SEREN** *notices* **CARYL** *approaching.*)

SEREN. God, I can't believe it's nearly lunchtime. You should have woken me.

> (**CARYL** *joins them, passing* **SEREN** *a cup of tea just as Meirion's phone beeps from somewhere.*)

MEIRION. Where the hell is that then?

> (*He checks in his pockets, on the table and then around the room.* **CARYL** *and* **SEREN** *watch this performance.* **SEREN** *takes out her phone and calls him.*)

SEREN. I'm ringing it now, dad.

> (*His phone rings continuously, until finally he pulls it out of a lobster pot but forgets what he wanted it for in the first place.*)

CARYL. Who was it?

> (*He looks at the screen.*)

MEIRION. Seren.

CARYL. No, the message you old bugger.

MEIRION. Oh, right.

(Looks at his phone again.)

The Normans.

SEREN. The Normans?

CARYL. I know, you couldn't make it up! Max and Jenny Norman. The new ones next door. Normans out there and *(Pointing to **SEREN**'s tummy.)* a Viking in here.

MEIRION. *(Reading.) Hello Meirion –* at least he can spell it *– hope all is well by the sea. I forgot to tell you we've had an alarm put in. So, if you do need to go over there for anything the code is 237890. And the builder called, they're starting early, should be there tomorrow morning. Exciting! Thanks a mill. Max. Thumbs up, rainbow, peace sign.*

SEREN. He sounds nice.

CARYL. He's one of those cold-water swimming nut cases. But he eats a lot of your dad's crab, so he likes him. Not met her yet.

*(**MEIRION** looks for a pen.)*

MEIRION. He's a good sort. And Caryl, you did meet her once.

CARYL. No, I never. So, the builders start tomorrow. So much for the peace and quiet.

(He finds a pen and writes the code on his hand.)

CARYL. What are you writing that code on your hand for?

MEIRION. Shouldn't you be on your way to Angharad's by now?

CARYL. I almost forgot! Seren, I'm so sorry to do this but I promised Angharad that I'd go over there today. You're not back off to Cardiff just yet, are you?

SEREN. No. I thought I'd stay a couple more days.

(**MEIRION** *heads off into the hall.*)

CARYL. Grand.

SEREN. If that's okay?

CARYL. Of course, it is. I might even get used to that *(Pointing to **SEREN**'s bump.)* by then. Are you sure you don't mind me going?

SEREN. No, it's fine mam. Honestly. I'll keep Dad company.

CARYL. Right, I'll need to head off if I'm going to catch the twelve twenty-eight.

(**SEREN** *looks at her watch.*)

SEREN. You won't make it mam, that new stop is a half hour walk at least.

CARYL. I'll put a sprint on. Life in the old girl yet.

SEREN. Bugger the bus, I'll give you a lift.

CARYL. Are you sure?

SEREN. It's fine, of course it's fine. You want to go right now?

CARYL. I'll sort this mess later. Thanks love. We can have a chat in the car.

SEREN. *(Uncertain.)* About what?

CARYL. About you becoming a *mammy*.

SEREN. Or you, becoming a Nain. Or would you prefer Mamgu?

CARYL. My own grandchild and I still feel like a little girl myself.

SEREN. I just need a quick wee.

(**SEREN** *exits into the toilet.* **MEIRION** *enters with his boots on and pulling a jumper over his head.*)

CARYL. Seren's giving me a lift there and I'll get Angharad to drop me back but it won't be until late. Where are you off?

MEIRION. Nowhere.

> (**CARYL** *grabs Gareth's business card from the side.*)

CARYL. Right. Okay, well, I was thinking, if I get chance, I'll stop by and see that estate agent in town. Let him know we're serious.

> *(Blackout.)*

ACT TWO

Scene One

(Later that evening.)

(Rain and wind batter the house, as if the outside is trying to make its way in.)

*(**MEIRION** sits at the kitchen table with the bottle of whiskey that Max gave him open, nursing his third, maybe fourth glass. On the table opposite him, propped up against a lobster pot, is a painting which is facing him but away from the audience.)*

*(**CARYL**, has just come in through the front door and stands with her coat on and holding two large paint containers.)*

MEIRION. What's with the paint?

CARYL. Angharad's new fella gave it to me.

MEIRION. Why?

CARYL. He's a decorator. Nice bloke too. Said we could have these for free. He's got loads of it left over from all the jobs he's been doing over winter. They give him the money upfront, but he always happens to buy just a bit too much. All top notch stuff. He normally flogs it.

MEIRION. I mean, why have *you* got it?

CARYL. Just thought we should spruce the place up a bit.

MEIRION. Really?

CARYL. It's going to need it.

MEIRION. We're not going anywhere Caryl.

CARYL. No? Well, I am, I'm off to bed.

MEIRION. *(Pointing to the picture.)* Don't you want to know what this is?

CARYL. *(Ignoring him.)* Where's Seren?

MEIRION. Asleep. Caryl, I asked you a question. I said, don't you want to know what this is?

CARYL. Looks like a painting from where I'm standing.

MEIRION. Clever Caryl. Don't you want to know where it came from?

CARYL. Not really. Look Meirion, I'm / knackered.

MEIRION. Thought I'd check on Max's place for him.

CARYL. Why?

MEIRION. Something playing on my mind. A feeling I just couldn't shake.

CARYL. Right.

MEIRION. And then I found this. In the loft.

CARYL. What were you doing in his loft?

MEIRION. I was being neighbourly Caryl.

CARYL. Neighbourly?

MEIRION. The art of being a good neighbour. You know it well I believe. Where do you think we should put it?

CARYL. Sorry?

MEIRION. I'm asking you where we should put up this picture that our dearly departed friend and neighbour Glyn painted. Or *Glyndŵr* as I see he signed it just here.

CARYL. You could get in trouble snooping around in other people's houses. And that's not yours to take. Didn't Max say that he'd asked Glyn's Owen to pick up all the left-over stuff.

MEIRION. You think Owen would want to see this?

CARYL. I've no idea what his feelings are on art / but

MEIRION. Or on nudes?

> (**MEIRION** *turns the picture round so it is now visible to the audience. It is a nude of a woman in her fifties. The face of the woman isn't visible.*)

CARYL. Not a clue.

MEIRION. You don't think this would float his boat? Tickle his pickle?

CARYL. Don't be absurd.

MEIRION. What about Glyn's pickle?

CARYL. I'm off to bed / now.

> (**MEIRION** *blocks* **CARYL**'s *exit.*)

MEIRION. Caryl, I'm asking if you knew what tickled Glyn's pickle. He painted it after all.

CARYL. You obviously don't like it. So, just take it back over there will you.

MEIRION. The problem is, I can't stop staring at it. It has a certain hold over me.

CARYL. I'll take it then.

MEIRION. No, hold on. You know, I think perhaps I don't know enough about art. Never did. Never took the time to learn.

CARYL. I don't think you'd be that interested. Not really your thing.

MEIRION. Well, I've got a good idea, how about you give me a little lesson now? A beginner's guide.

CARYL. At ten o'clock at night? Don't be weird. And you're half cut.

MEIRION. Am I? Come and have a drink with me then. Enlighten me about the wonderful world of modern art.

CARYL. Maybe tomorrow night *if* there's any left.

MEIRION. Come on, Caryl. Be nice. For once.

CARYL. I'm beyond tired right now. Let me get off.

MEIRION. No. I want to learn all about this magnificent painting. And I want to learn now.

> (**CARYL** *hesitates. She knows she can't escape so decides to humour him, a change in her plan.* **MEIRION** *pours her a glass of whiskey, they lock eyes but don't sit, they move around the room.*)

I always thought Glyn just did local landscapes.

CARYL. Most of the time.

MEIRION. But not all the time.

CARYL. He was intrigued by what a natural landscape could tell you about the people from that place. And I guess the same could be said for that picture.

> (**CARYL** *pushes her glass across the table and* **MEIRION** *pours her another drink. She looks at the painting and smiles.*)

Glyn always said you should think of a body like a landscape, you know. Look at it. If you look closely, you can see all the lakes and the rivers, the mountains and the shorelines. He was fascinated by what a body could tell you about its environment. What's its story? What's that body been through, you know?

(**MEIRION** *moves closer to the picture, looking very closely at it and then back at* **CARYL**.)

MEIRION. *(Venomously.)* Your tits look much better than that in real life, you do know that?

(Silence and then **CARYL** *starts laughing.)*

CARYL. You think that's me?

MEIRION. Think?

CARYL. You're saying that's me?

MEIRION. I know that's you.

CARYL. That's just. You've. How much have you had to drink?

MEIRION. I said I *know* that's you.

CARYL. You're being ridiculous.

MEIRION. Do you know, how I know?

CARYL. Totally lost it now, haven't you.

MEIRION. Do you know, how I know?

CARYL. It's the stress of everything. Seren turning up pregnant. All this Government stuff. All this talk of moving, I'm sorry if I've upset you.

MEIRION. Upset me?

CARYL. I really think the best thing would be for you to get some sleep. You've not been sleeping well, I know / that.

MEIRION. Let me tell you, Caryl. Let me tell you how I know that's you in that painting. Apart from the fact that I know what my own wife's body looks / like.

CARYL. This is madness.

MEIRION. This time two years ago, when you were in hospital for your gallbladder, he came over here, and he told me some home truths, he did. Pissed as a fart he was. An old drunk cunt. An old drunk Welsh cunt. In his stupid artist's get up and that ridiculous beret, he wore.

CARYL. Meirion, come on love. You're getting yourself worked up over nothing.

MEIRION. You have no idea.

> (**MEIRION** *pours himself another large whiskey and downs it in one.*)

CARYL. Look, whatever he said to / you

MEIRION. You know what he said to me, don't you?

CARYL. I've not got a clue, but I'm sure whatever / it

MEIRION. You know.

CARYL. Stop this now Meirion. I don't like it.

MEIRION. You know. You know. I know you know.

CARYL. This isn't you.

MEIRION. Are you going to say it, or shall I?

(He stares at her, hard, until she turns away.)

(Agonised.) He told me that you were having an affair.

CARYL. An affair?

MEIRION. That's right.

CARYL. With who?

MEIRION. With him! Fucking Pound-shop Picasso.

CARYL. What?

MEIRION. That you'd been screwing each other behind my back.

CARYL. *(Laughing.)* Come on.

MEIRION. Whenever I went out on the boat, you'd be round there like a shot, he said.

CARYL. Meirion. That's / preposterous.

MEIRION. Like a rat up a drainpipe, he said.

CARYL. Why on earth would Glyn have said that? This is just / madness.

MEIRION. Don't I deserve to know the truth? Look at me Caryl.

> *(Pause. She looks at him and then* **CARYL** *picks up the picture and studies it. The radio turns on, very quietly to start and then building throughout the scene.)*

CARYL. It wasn't like that.

MEIRION. I knew it! I didn't believe it, but I guess I always fucking knew it. Lonely, were you? Living here. Bit of attention from the old master next door and pulled your knickers straight down did you?

CARYL. No. It's not what you think. I let him paint me like that / but

MEIRION. So that is you! I thought you said it wasn't you?

CARYL. It's not.

MEIRION. Yes, it is.

CARYL. No.

> *(***MEIRION** *becomes angry and emotional whilst* **CARYL** *maintains her composure.)*

MEIRION. Caryl, that is you!

CARYL. No, Meirion. It's not me.

MEIRION. Are you taking the piss out of me? Is that what the pair of you did together? Laughed at me behind my back?

CARYL. I know you *think* that's me.

MEIRION. I know that's you.

CARYL. It's a different me.

MEIRION. A different you?

CARYL. That's not me. This is me, here now. That's just a painting, of a *different* me.

*(A rage grows inside **MEIRION**, and he knocks over a chair and stuff from the table.)*

MEIRION. *(Screams.)* Caryl! What the fuck have you done?

(He stares at the painting in his hands.)

CARYL. Meirion! Keep your voice down. Seren is asleep upstairs, remember?

MEIRION. *(Quieter now.)* Then tell me what happened.

CARYL. I'm not sure I can.

MEIRION. You just need to try a bit harder now.

CARYL. I don't think you'd understand.

MEIRION. Try me.

CARYL. It's complicated.

MEIRION. Complicated. How?

CARYL. I didn't have an affair with Glyn but *(Pointing at the painting.)* she did.

MEIRION. *(Laughing.)* You must think I'm a right mug.

CARYL. No. You just don't know that person is all.

MEIRION. How dare you. I've known you since you were fifteen years old.

CARYL. I'm sorry Meirion. It's not what you think.

MEIRION. You're lots of things Caryl but I never had you down as a cheat.

CARYL. It wasn't like that.

MEIRION. All these years we've spent here together. Everything we've faced, we've done it together.

CARYL. Glyn knew me in a way you didn't.

MEIRION. Oh right!

CARYL. A different version of me. A me that even I didn't realise existed. Being with him was different, that's all.

MEIRION. That's what you wanted was it? Different!

CARYL. No. I didn't want it. I needed it. To escape.

MEIRION. So, he was telling the truth after all.

> (**CARYL** *nods. She takes the picture out of his hands and puts it on the table.*)

CARYL. I'm sorry Meirion. It wasn't anything. It was a few weeks of. Nothing.

MEIRION. Nothing? You destroyed us, you destroyed our family, for nothing?

CARYL. It's like it wasn't even me doing it. I never wanted to do that. It wasn't like I was looking for it. Honestly. I promise. Please believe me.

MEIRION. Believe you? *Now* you want me to believe you? You've been lying to me all this time.

CARYL. If I could. If I could stop her. Stop me. From doing that. I didn't love him. I didn't. I'm so sorry.

MEIRION. Sorry I found out?

CARYL. No. Sorry for what I've done to you. To us.

MEIRION. So, there we are / then

CARYL. Meirion / please.

MEIRION. I've tried to forget. Tried to move on. Who was I kidding? See I just knew. I knew I had to get over there. I had to go there tonight. Just to see. Before it was too late. To see if what he'd said was true. He told me he'd painted you, see. Like *that*. And I had to know. To know what you'd done. To know what I'd done. Do you have any idea, Caryl? What it's been like. These past two years. Agony. I've been in *agony*. I told myself it couldn't, *couldn't* be true. But what's worse, if it is true or not? I still don't know. Even now I don't know. Does it make it worse, or does it make it better? The *guilt*. The fucking guilt. Gnawing away at me. But it's true. All true. You were carrying on with him, just like he said.

> *(Pause.)*

CARYL. What do you mean by *guilt*, Meirion?

> *(Pause.)*

What exactly have you got to feel *guilty* about?

> *(Pause.* **MEIRION** *suddenly appears more dangerous to her.)*

MEIRION. Penny not dropped yet, Caryl?

CARYL. *(Laughing.)* Don't be so stupid.

MEIRION. What was I meant to do?

CARYL. You're not being serious.

MEIRION. Meant to just suck that up was I? Same old Meirion. Never any trouble.

CARYL. Stop this now Meirion.

MEIRION. Doing that to you. The only woman I've ever loved.

CARYL. This can't be true.

MEIRION. What, you don't think I've got it in me?

CARYL. Have you hell.

MEIRION. No?

CARYL. You wouldn't hurt a fly.

MEIRION. I bash the brains out of fish all the time. What makes you think I couldn't bash Glyn's brains in?

CARYL. Because that's not who you are.

MEIRION. Well, maybe there's another version of *me* too. A version you don't know. A version you wouldn't like.

CARYL. *(Mocking.)* What, so you pushed him off the top of that cliff did you?

MEIRION. No. I did it here. Just by here. And now he's out there. All alone, deep, deep down in the dirt. In my family's garden. *(Now full of rage.)* So, if you think we're *ever* fucking selling this place you've got another thing coming.

> *(CARYL stares at MEIRION for a moment before looking out the back window. She opens the back door and soil starts to pour in from outside. She turns to stare at MEIRION for a moment, then turns away again and runs.)*
>
> *(MEIRION is left alone as the soil continues to pour in. The radio, which has built to a painful cacophony of distorted sound, fills the room with noise.)*
>
> *(Blackout.)*

Interval

Scene Two

(A few hours later.)

(The storm has passed but the room remains in a state of disarray.)

*(**MAX** enters through the open back door.)*

*(**MEIRION**, just now awake from sleeping on the sofa, sits looking groggy. Fully dressed, shoes off by the side of the sofa and a blanket draped over him. **MAX** suddenly notices him.)*

MAX. I thought I saw someone.

MEIRION. What? Where?

MAX. In your back garden.

MEIRION. When?

MAX. As I drove in, just now.

MEIRION. Who was it?

MAX. I don't know. I thought maybe it was you.

MEIRION. I was asleep, on here. You just woke me.

MAX. Sorry, I was just worried something might have happened.

MEIRION. Happened?

MAX. For the door to be left open like that. At this time. In this weather. The storm, it's turned this place upside down.

MEIRION. What time is it?

MAX. Four a.m. Just after.

MEIRION. Christ. What a mess.

MAX. Let me help.

MEIRION. Thank you Max.

MAX. Dim problem.

> *(They start to put the room back together.* **MEIRION** *notices* **MAX** *picking up the near empty bottle of whiskey.)*

Big night was it?

MEIRION. Seren, our daughter, is here. We just found out she's having a baby!

MAX. Ah, that's awesome.

MEIRION. Thanks.

MAX. You must be thrilled.

MEIRION. Yes, our first grandchild!

MAX. Well, I'm chuffed for you. And Caryl.

> *(They continue to tidy in silence for a moment.)*

MEIRION. What are you doing here, Max?

MAX. Well, I saw the door was open / and I just

MEIRION. No. I mean what are you doing *here*. In Porth Y Graith. At four a.m. You only left on Friday. I thought you weren't back until May.

MAX. Jenny and I. Well, we've. We've had a bit of a row. So, I thought it best if I, you know, if I gave her some space.

MEIRION. Women, eh!

MAX. Yeah.

> *(**MAX** picks up some photos which have been knocked over.)*

Who's this?

MEIRION. That's my grandparents. Dai the Fish and Megan, or Mrs Dai the Fish. He was born here in, erm, in 1915.

MAX. That's wild.

MEIRION. It's changed a hell of a lot, mind. Not the house so much, but this village.

MAX. Was your father a fisher too?

MEIRION. Oh yes, but you know, round here, we would do a bit of everything to get by. You know this place was even a bit of a BnB at one time. That's how I met Caryl actually. She was down here with her family.

MAX. *(Amused.)* Caryl met you here on her *holidays*?

MEIRION. Tickled you, has it? She came down with her parents from Tregaron, three summers on the trot. She was something else. When she agreed to move here, I couldn't believe my luck. Her *here*, with *me*. I was over the moon.

(Beat.)

MAX. Jenny and I. Today. Yesterday. We went out for a late brunch. This place she likes. The food is amazing. And we always have the same thing. Every time we have the same thing. I have the 'nduja eggs and she has the roasted mushrooms on focaccia. But yesterday, we got there, and she said she wanted the Ricotta Pancake.

MEIRION. A Ricotta Pancake?

MAX. Yeah. A Ricotta Pancake. Which was weird, because she's never once had that before. Then just as the food came, she told me she was leaving me. I was in a bit of a dark place when my dad died last year, you know, but we'd worked through it, I thought everything was getting better. And moving here. Having the place down here. It was meant to be a new start. A new chapter. For *us*. But she, she wants to be alone. I don't think I'll ever be able to eat 'nduja with eggs again.

MEIRION. I'm so sorry Max.

MAX. Nah, it's fine, I mean, no, I am pretty devastated to be honest. So, I came here. I think I just wanted to be here, by the sea. *(Beat.)* I don't have any photos of my grandparents.

MEIRION. Are they still alive?

>   (**MAX** *shakes his head.*)

MAX. My dad's parents died when he was young. My mum was from Zambia. Lusaka. But she died about five years ago. But the celebrations every time we went back, the ritual, and the ceremony. Like I don't mean to be rude, but here we just don't do that, you know. That level of *joy*. I loved it. But then, you know, my Mbuya, my grandmother, when she'd put me to bed at night, she'd always tuck me in super tight, I loved that and then she'd give me the biggest kiss and say, "goodnight my little white prince" *(Beat.)* And that was hard. How they saw me, it was hard. I didn't say anything to anyone, didn't want to stress Mum out I guess, but I just didn't know what to do with that, especially, you know, because then obviously over here, growing up in Chepstow things were like, well you know.

MEIRION. *(Surprised.)* Chepstow?

>   (*A smile spreads across* **MAX**'s *face.*)

MAX. Ha ha! I know right. I've been waiting for the right time to drop that bombshell. But I imagine that down here you don't quite count Chepstow as actual Wales?

MEIRION. Oh, I don't know about that! Depends on what part of the town you live in, doesn't it? Or what century you're in.

>   (*Pause.* **MEIRION** *goes down on his knees to pick some bits up.* **MAX** *picks up the painting from the table.*)

MAX. I've seen this before. Was it not in my loft?

(**MEIRION** *turns to look at* **MAX.**)

MEIRION. It was as it happens. *(Beat.)* Now, I hope you don't mind. I just wanted to, with the storm coming, you know, with the storm, I thought I should check all your windows were closed, tight. When it gets bad down here, the smallest gap and they can come clean off. So, I went over, and I thought, when I was there, I thought I heard something up there. In your loft. We've had rats before, you know, up in our roof, total nightmare, so thought I'd better check.

MAX. I've got rats? In my roof!

MEIRION. No, no, you're fine, false alarm, must have just been the wind picking up. But yeah, I saw *that*, and I know I should have asked but I just thought Caryl might want to take a look, you know.

MAX. Does she like it?

MEIRION. She does.

MAX. Okay.

MEIRION. Not so keen myself. Take it back with you.

MAX. No, no, if Caryl likes it, you should keep it.

(**MAX** *puts the painting down just as the back door flings open and* **CARYL**, *soaking wet and cold, rushes into the room, out of breath; she's desperate to speak to* **MEIRION** *but she sees* **MAX** *and freezes.*)

Caryl!

CARYL. Hello Max.

MAX. I thought you were in bed!

CARYL. I thought you were in Bristol.

MAX. No, I had to. Jenny and I. We're just. Long story! You're soaked to the bone.

MEIRION. Max was just helping me clean up down here.

CARYL. Right.

MEIRION. The back door was open, and the storm ripped right through the place.

CARYL. That must have been me, who left it open. I had to go up to the site. Thanks for your help Max. I can take over now.

MAX. Are you sure?

CARYL. Go to bed Max.

MAX. Right, well. Okay. I could do with some zeds.

CARYL. Nos da.

MAX. Nos da.

(MAX goes. MEIRION and CARYL stare at each other for a moment.)

MEIRION. Caryl. Caryl can / we

CARYL. I'm sorry Meirion. For leaving like that. For leaving you like that. I'm so sorry.

MEIRION. What I / said.

CARYL. I shouldn't have gone.

MEIRION. Keeping all that from / you.

CARYL. But I'm back now.

MEIRION. Knowing he was out there. Wondering if you were yearning after him.

(CARYL shakes her head.)

CARYL. I didn't think you loved me, Meirion. I thought we were just trapped together, you know.

MEIRION. Trapped together?

CARYL. I can't remember the last time you touched me. It's been *years*. I thought that was it. That you didn't want me anymore. But, I was wrong, wasn't I?

MEIRION. Bloody hell, Caryl! It took me murdering a man to convince you that I loved you?

CARYL. You didn't *murder* him.

MEIRION. I can promise you that he is very much dead and under that shed outside.

CARYL. He might be dead, but I don't believe for one second that you murdered him.

MEIRION. He arrived here that night, pockets *full* of booze. I was so worried about you in hospital, see, I thought some company might help.

I took him at cards, three games on the trot and he got up to leave. Then, he started to fill the room with stories of you, the colour of your eyes, how he'd always like to watch you when you'd dry yourself down on the beach, what your arse looked like as you walked up the hill towards the site. He asked me if I liked the painting that he'd done of you, knowing full well that I'd never seen it. He said for a such an old bitch, you were a surprisingly obedient subject. And I couldn't just... *(Deep sigh.)* Look, I'm going to get this fire going, warm you up a bit.

> (**MEIRION** *builds the fire and* **CARYL** *peels off her wet clothes whilst listening to* **MEIRION**.)

It was just two old drunk blokes pushing each other around really, moving towards each other and then backing away, snapping our claws at each other. More desperate to stay upright than to take the other one down. Then suddenly this stream of vile liquid sprayed across my face. The dirty old bastard had spat at me.

Asked me if I could, if I could taste you. *(Beat.)* If I could, I'd have battered him to death, but he stumbled back away from me and fell over that bloody step. Flipped over on his back, the pathetic beast. Fuck him I thought. Fuck him. Fuck him. And I was ready for him, I had my dukes up, whatever that bastard had for me, I was ready. *(Beat.)* But he didn't get up. Smashed his head here see and then all this blood just started to pour out of him. Out of his mouth. What he said about you Caryl. Here in our home.

> *(**MEIRION** takes off his jumper and gives it to **CARYL** so they both appear half dressed.)*

He made this noise. I'll never forget it. I stayed with him until he'd gone, then I ran out into the night. But I was the only one here. Everyone else gone now. Not a single other living soul here to see what I'd done.

> *(**MEIRION** lights a match and gets the fire going.)*

I thought about calling for help but no way an ambulance could have got all the way out here in time. And what would I say to the police? That it was an accident? They might have believed me, there was enough booze in him to sink a trawler. But then, I stopped myself. See, what if, what if what he'd said about you *was* true? And what if other people knew? I wasn't going to let them point their fingers at me. So, I put him to rest here. Safer that way. But he's not at rest, is he? He's still here with us. And the thoughts of you and him together have haunted me ever since.

CARYL. I wasn't in love with him. I didn't even like him that much. *(Beat.)* Look, Meirion, I've been so stupid. I can see that now but, I need you to listen to me okay. I need to. I have to tell you something.

MEIRION. About you and him?

CARYL. I've been trying to make sense of it. Why the hell I did it. Why did that happen. And it's not an excuse but *(Beat.)* there's something I've been keeping from you.

MEIRION. What?

CARYL. I am not.

(Pause.)

MEIRION. You're not what?

CARYL. Welsh. *(Beat.)* I am not Welsh.

MEIRION. What?

CARYL. Not fully.

MEIRION. Sorry?

CARYL. I'm half Welsh.

MEIRION. What's the other half?

(**CARYL** *hangs her head in shame.*)

CARYL. *(Whispers.)* English.

MEIRION. Sorry?

CARYL. *(Louder now.)* English!

MEIRION. You're half English? You?

CARYL. I'm sorry Meirion. I'm so sorry.

MEIRION. Caryl, I've just told you I killed a man!

CARYL. I was born in England.

MEIRION. Am I meant to be finding this funny?

CARYL. London.

MEIRION. Are you actually serious?

CARYL. And my dad was from Kent.

MEIRION. Your parents were from Tregaron!

(**CARYL** *shakes her head.*)

CARYL. My mother was from Machynlleth, but she moved to London for work, where she met my dad. But she died young. She had cancer and it took her away from us so quickly.

MEIRION. *(Confused.)* When was this?

CARYL. She died three days after my seventh birthday. And my father, well, he just couldn't cope. I was sent to live with my mother's sister and her husband back here in Wales. Just whilst he recovered, everyone said. That's who you knew as my parents.

MEIRION. I had no idea.

CARYL. They'd been trying for years to have their own children. And they were amazing. They made me feel safe and wanted. Wales made me feel safe and wanted. They used to only row in Welsh, so I wouldn't know what they were saying, they didn't want to unsettle me. But by the time I was eleven my Welsh was better than theirs. They became my mam and dad and Wales became my home. My magic coat of armour. There was no way then that anyone would have known they weren't my real parents, so when we moved to Tregaron for Dad's work, we didn't feel the need to tell anyone any different. We didn't ever discuss it again.

MEIRION. What about your father? Your *real* father?

CARYL. He never asked for me back.

MEIRION. And you never told me that.

CARYL. That my own father didn't *want* me?

MEIRION. You should have told me.

CARYL. Wales has always been...*me* I suppose. And I was terrified of telling you that I wasn't *that*. That I wasn't *me*. It became a mountain in my mind. I didn't tell anyone.

MEIRION. Apart from Glyn?

CARYL. He found out.

MEIRION. How?

CARYL. The DVLA.

MEIRION. What?

CARYL. Glyn's son.

MEIRION. Owen?

CARYL. No, the nasty little one. Ianto. He works at the DVLA these days. He was processing my provisional driving licence after they stopped the bus. Phoned his dad in hysterics because the mad lady from next door who always used to shout *sdim parch da ti y diawl bach!* was born in London.

MEIRION. Had a right laugh, did they?

CARYL. He asked if you knew. I didn't know what to say. I was petrified that he'd tell you.

MEIRION. What did you think I'd do?

CARYL. Laugh at me. Leave me. I thought it would be a good excuse for you to finally be rid of me. I couldn't think straight. I couldn't handle the shame. The shame of being unwanted. Of being a liar. When you've buried something like that inside yourself for so long.

MEIRION. But that doesn't explain, why you / had to

CARYL. He agreed not to say anything to you. Not to mention it in front of you. And once I started to talk about it with him, I just couldn't stop. *Finally,* I could talk about what I'd lost. About the pain. How sometimes I thought I could still almost smell my mother. And that all I ever really wanted was for my father to tell me he loved me.

*(**CARYL** picks up the picture and traces her fingers over it.)*

Suddenly I felt free. I feel sick to my stomach saying it now, but Glyn allowed me to see a different version of myself and that little girl inside, that I'd buried deep within myself, who had never been allowed to become a woman, she finally managed to escape. Suddenly, she could feel the sun on her face. She could swim in the sea and trace pictures in the sand. She could feel who she might have been, and she felt wanted and desired. I felt wanted and desired. To be painted like that, just to *exist*. I should never have done it, but I just felt I had to escape.

MEIRION. From me?

CARYL. From myself.

*(**CARYL** takes the picture and holds in her hands.)*

CARYL. I wondered what had happened to her. I thought about going over there. See if she was still there. But the thought of being in that house. I couldn't. I just couldn't. Diolch for bringing her back to me. She's mine now, not his.

When I came out of the hospital, and he was gone, I was relieved. I wanted nothing more than to be left alone in our home, back in my own bed, in *our* bed. What I had with him wasn't ever real. I've been stuck at sea for years and I just liked the feeling of suddenly being someone else. I felt different in my own skin, I thought I deserved just a little moment in the sun. I didn't care that I might get burned.

MEIRION. And now?

CARYL. I guess, now *(Beat.)* now, I'm home.

MEIRION. With me?

CARYL. You are my home, Meirion.

> (**CARYL** *moves towards* **MEIRION**. **MEIRION** *holds* **CARYL** *as she rests her head on his chest.* **MEIRION** *looks around the room.*)

MEIRION. I'll go to the police.

CARYL. You can't.

MEIRION. No more lies.

CARYL. You'll go to prison.

MEIRION. I know.

CARYL. And I'd be stuck here by myself.

MEIRION. Not here. Best we sell after all. Be rid of this place. Be rid of it all.

CARYL. That doesn't matter now. None of that matters now.

MEIRION. Get you away from here.

CARYL. But I'd be more alone than ever.

MEIRION. I know. I'm sorry.

CARYL. You can't

MEIRION. Caryl. I have to. Now you know what happened, I have to. I won't have you implicated.

CARYL. This is as much my mess as yours.

MEIRION. Caryl. I'm not a religious man. I don't talk to God. I'm not even sure there is a God. But sometimes, if I listen hard enough, I can hear the voices of my family in these walls. And that's enough for me. I know what I have to do. You and Seren. I need to protect you both from all of this. I did this and I'm not scared of the consequences. Not anymore. *(Beat.)* But after the baby comes, okay? I'll do it after the baby is here. I want Seren to bring her here. So, I can see her here. I want my family to see her here.

CARYL. Please Meirion. Let's just talk about it again. You're tired now. We can talk about it again, okay? Please, go get some rest and we'll talk about it / again.

MEIRION. Caryl, look at me.

CARYL. You're tired.

MEIRION. It's going to be okay. I'll make it right.

CARYL. We'll talk about it again. You go up now. I won't be long.

>   (**MEIRION** *nods and heads upstairs.*)
>
>   (*Now by herself,* **CARYL** *takes the painting in her hands.*)

CARYL. (*To the painting.*) What the hell were you thinking?

>   (*Suddenly the radio turns on by itself, startling* **CARYL** *for a moment, then she walks over to it and pulls the plug out before sticking it in a cupboard.*)

Paid.*

SEREN. (*Calling from upstairs.*) Mam?

>   (**CARYL** *quickly puts the picture away.*)

CARYL. Morning love.

SEREN. You're up early.

CARYL. There's been a storm.

SEREN. Really?

CARYL. The back door was open. The place was a right state. But we seem to have things under control now. Your dad's just gone back to bed.

SEREN. I didn't hear a thing!

---

* English: *Don't.*

CARYL. Probably for the best.

SEREN. Have you been crying?

CARYL. No.

SEREN. Yes, you have.

CARYL. No. Just been getting the fire going is all. Warm the old place up.

SEREN. This place. It just sends me into such a deep sleep.

CARYL. No love, that's the drugs we've been putting in your food.

SEREN. Are you sure you're okay? Do you want a drink or something?

CARYL. I was just thinking I might try and close my eyes for a bit. You're not up for the day already, are you?

SEREN. I went to bed at eight thirty last night. Not sure how much more sleep one person can have.

CARYL. But you're sleeping for two! I'll stay up, keep you company.

SEREN. No. Go get some rest. Honestly, I'll be fine. Be light soon.

>   (**CARYL** *kisses* **SEREN** *on the head.*)

What's that for?

CARYL. Do I need an excuse?

>   (**CARYL** *goes upstairs.* **SEREN** *warms herself by the fire.*)

>   (*A gentle knock at the back door.* **SEREN** *is startled.*)

MAX. (*From outside.*) Hello.

SEREN. Hello?

MAX. *(From outside.)* Are you still up?

SEREN. Sorry?

MAX. *(From outside.)* It's Max.

SEREN. Max?

MAX. *(From outside.)* From next door.

>   (**SEREN** *opens the door.*)

SEREN. Oh yes, the Norman Invader!

MAX. Sorry?

SEREN. Just a joke.

MAX. Oh right. You must be. Like mother, like daughter. Look, I'm really sorry but I left my keys with Marion. Well, the spare keys but then I left *my* keys back at home.

SEREN. Marion?

MAX. Oh, God, no. Not again.

SEREN. It's okay.

MAX. It's not.

SEREN. Don't worry, honestly.

MAX. I just can't seem / to

SEREN. Repeat after me. Mey

MAX. I can't.

SEREN. You can do this.

MAX. Honestly, I don't think I can.

SEREN. Max. I believe in you. Come on. We've got this. Repeat after me. Mey.

MAX. Mey

SEREN. Ree

MAX. Ree

SEREN. On

MAX. On

SEREN. Mey. Ree. On. Meirion.

MAX. Mey. Ree. On. Meirion. Meirion. Meirion.

SEREN. Not that hard, was it? Let me have a look for these keys. Did you just get here?

MAX. No, I got here an hour or so ago. I saw your parents, *Meirion* and Caryl, when I got in, dealing with the storm damage, then when I got back over to mine, I realised that I was key-less. I didn't want to come straight back over again and disturb them. I can tell they already think I'm a bit much. People do. So, I just thought I'd sleep in the camper van and then come round again in the morning. But it is proper Baltic in there.

SEREN. Dad had them yesterday. Let me think.

MAX. Hey, congrats *(Pointing at her pregnant belly.)* by the way, on / the

SEREN. Oh, yeah, right. Thanks.

(**SEREN** *looks for the keys.*)

MAX. Look, it's a bit weird but can I ask you a question?

SEREN. I'm five months. That's why I'm already this big. I only just told my parents this weekend because I'm having it solo, by choice, using a sperm donor and I just knew it would freak them out, worried I'd disappoint them in some way I guess, so I kept putting it off and putting it off and putting off. But that's the thing about babies you can't keep it a secret forever – it's going to come out soon enough, quite literally.

MAX. Right. No. I mean, that's brilliant for you. Like wow, really brave.

SEREN. Thanks.

MAX. But, no, actually it was, it was something else.

SEREN. Oh God, sorry.

MAX. It's fine.

SEREN. Me, me, me.

MAX. No. I just mean. I wasn't. It's not like. I didn't want you to think I was staring at you or anything.

SEREN. Just going on about myself all the time.

MAX. I mean, if it makes you feel better, I did actually wonder why you were like so big already. I just wouldn't have dared ask.

SEREN. I've just kept it all a secret for so long, a relief to be able to tell people now, I guess. And I don't want it to be a secret, you know. From now on, I'm all about transparency.

MAX. Yeah, I mean. You shouldn't. You *should* tell people.

SEREN. Felt good to tell Mam and Dad. Finally. Biggest scandal that's ever happened to our family, that's for sure. Whatever will the neighbours say?

MAX. Well, as one of the actual neighbours, I can inform you that I think it's really cool.

*(****SEREN*** smiles.)*

SEREN. So, what was it?

MAX. What?

SEREN. That you actually wanted to ask.

MAX. Oh right, yeah. You know your mum.

SEREN. I've had the pleasure.

MAX. I kind of get the idea, that Caryl. Well, she's made it blindingly obvious actually that she's not too happy about. That she feels uncomfortable about the fact / that

SEREN. About you buying next door?

MAX. Right so, but like that's done now. And we are neighbours, so in your experience, how long should I expect her to be pissed off with me?

SEREN. That all depends.

MAX. On what?

SEREN. There's a sliding scale of hostility for incomers. The more you're here, the more she'll warm to you. She's a pussycat really. Why don't you come round for tea later, I'll get you on her good side in no time.

*(**SEREN** finds the keys and passes them to **MAX**.)*

Here they are.

MAX. Magic! Thank you so much. And yes please, amazing, I'd love that. Diolch. Hold on. Let me just. Meirion!

(Blackout.)

ACT THREE

Scene One

(Lights up on the house.)

(Warm sunny air fills the room.)

(The table is now clutter free, the painting is on the wall. The calendar now reads August. The back door is open.)

*(**SEREN**, no longer pregnant and carrying an overnight bag, stands facing **CARYL**.)*

CARYL. Where's my little Beti, then?

SEREN. *(With exaggerated sarcasm.)* Oh Hello Seren. How are you? So lovely to have you home.

CARYL. Oh, don't get all jealous now Seren. The sooner you accept that all the love I had for you has now transferred to your daughter, the better.

*(**MAX** enters carrying the baby in a car seat and passes it to **CARYL**.)*

MAX. Special Delivery.

SEREN. He insisted on carrying her.

*(**CARYL** puts the car seat on the table and stares adoringly at her grandchild.)*

CARYL. *(To Beti.)* Hello Cariad bach.

MAX. I was only following orders from your mother.

CARYL. You've had major abdominal surgery, love. Diolch yn fawr iawn Max for bringing them both here.

MAX. Croeso. I'll just go grab your cot.

(**MAX** *leaves.*)

CARYL. He's a good egg, isn't he.

SEREN. You've changed your tune.

CARYL. I only said he was a good egg. Don't get too excited. How was the journey? Beti alright?

SEREN. Good as gold.

CARYL. *(To Beti.)* Of course, you were. Oh, look at your little feet. Oh, my goodness. Your thighs are just. One roll, two roll, three roll, four. And that teeney tiny nose. And those ginormous eyes. Oh Beti. You beautiful, beautiful little thing. (**CARYL** *begins to cry.*) Oh God.

SEREN. You okay there, mam?

CARYL. Oh, you know. Just a bit emotional, having little Beti here, is all.

SEREN. *(Unconvinced.)* Right.

(**MAX** *comes back in carrying the cot.* **CARYL** *composes herself.*)

MAX. Looks like the Regatta is in full swing.

CARYL. Surprised you managed to find anywhere to park.

MAX. You entering into anything Caryl?

CARYL. Me?

MAX. Only, I was wondering, if you fancied doing the raft building with me?

CARYL. The raft race?

MAX. Looks epic.

CARYL. That's for children Max!

MAX. No, it's not.

CARYL. It is.

MAX. No. Anyone can enter.

CARYL. Don't be weird.

MAX. It said family event.

CARYL. But we're not family.

MAX. We're neighbours. Not far off. Come on, Caryl. Live a little.

CARYL. No way.

MAX. Os gwelwch yn dda.

CARYL. Stop it! Ask Seren. I'll look after Beti.

SEREN. I'm still recovering from *major* abdominal surgery, remember?

MAX. Caryl, please, please don't make me beg.

CARYL. You want me to build a raft with you?

MAX. Yes. And then race it.

CARYL. You're off your rocker.

MAX. I'll do most of the work Caryl. I promise. It's just, well, you can't enter by yourself. You have to have a team of at least two. And you do owe me a favour, bringing Seren and Beti down here in the van.

CARYL. You offered!

MAX. Serious detour that was. Added hours onto my day.

SEREN. See mam, you have to now. Be rude not to.

CARYL. I can't believe this is happening.

MAX. So, you'll do it?

CARYL. If it will stop you going on.

MAX. Get in! We are going to smash it.

CARYL. When is it?

MAX. In fifteen minutes.

CARYL. Better go get changed then I suppose. *(To Beti.)* See you in a minute my little Calon Cabatsien. What the hell have I got myself into.

> *(**CARYL** goes upstairs. **SEREN** moves over to Beti.)*

SEREN. I cannot believe she just said yes to that.

MAX. What did your mum just call Beti, heart something?

SEREN. Cabatsien? Cabbage.

MAX. Cabbage Heart?

SEREN. Funny when you say it like that. But it's what she always called me too.

> *(**SEREN** picks up Beti and outs her on her shoulder and walks around the room before looking out to sea.)*

When I was small, Mam used to tell me this story about a little girl who had lived all alone in the lime kilns, by there. Her mammy was taken away one night by an angry sea monster and her daddy got lost in the sea mist looking for her. So, she lived there, all by herself, hoping her daddy would find his way back to her one day. Only he never came. She was looked after by a pair of puffins, and you know the only thing she ate was cabbages. Maybe that's where that came from. Calon Cabatsien.

MAX. Poor little Calon Cabatsien.

SEREN. I know right. Proper tragic.

(**MAX** *points to the painting.*)

MAX. Hey, what do you think of this? Came out of my loft.

SEREN. It's horrible. Just like the prick who painted it.

MAX. Not one of his adoring fans, then?

SEREN. Sorry, I shouldn't have. That wasn't fair. You're living in his house.

MAX. Nah, it's fine. Anyway, by the time those builders finally finish there won't be any trace of him left. I even flogged the two pictures of his that Jen bought.

(**MAX** *notices* **SEREN** *looks visibly shaken.*)

Hey, are you okay?

SEREN. I'm fine.

MAX. Are you sure? You look like you've seen a ghost.

(**MEIRION** *enters.* **SEREN** *suddenly brightens.*)

MEIRION. Seren. You're here! Thank you, Max, for bringing them up.

SEREN. Hi dad!

MAX. A pleasure, Meirion. Right, I better head off, tell your mum I'll see her on the beach in ten.

(**MAX** *leaves.*)

SEREN. Max has convinced Mam to do the raft race with him.

MEIRION. What the hell is she doing that for?

SEREN. Max wouldn't take no for an answer. I think she's actually got a bit of a soft spot for him. Said he's a good egg. Is he down here a lot?

MEIRION. Most of the time now really. Since he and his wife went their separate ways.

SEREN. So, that's all final is it now?

MEIRION. It would appear so.

SEREN. Big change for him then. He didn't really talk about it on the way down here. How's he taken it?

> (**MEIRION** *doesn't respond.*)

Dad?

MEIRION. Sorry? Let me have a look at this little girl. She's doubled in size since I last saw her.

SEREN. That was only two weeks ago you were in Cardiff mind.

> (*Silence.* **MEIRION** *is lost in his thoughts.*)

You alright dad?

MEIRION. Oh, you know.

> (*Beti starts to cry.* **SEREN** *sniffs her bum.*)

SEREN. Oh no, not again.

> (**SEREN** *looks around the room.*)

And I've left the changing bag in the front of Max's van.

> (**SEREN** *thrusts Beti on* **MEIRION** *and exits.*)

> (**MEIRION** *walks around the room, holding Beti, trying to comfort her.*)

MEIRION. Hey come on now cariad. You're here with us now. We've been waiting for you. *I've* been waiting.

> (*Blackout.*)

Scene Two

(Later that day.)

*(**SEREN** is sat breastfeeding Beti.)*

*(**CARYL** and **MAX**, both wearing life jackets and with gold medals around their necks, each hold an oar.)*

MAX. I have to hand it to you Caryl, you were a bit slow to start but once you saw those next to / us

CARYL. The Swn Y Môr lot.

MAX. You put on a right spurt.

CARYL. Worth it to see their faces. Oh God, I needed that! Worked off a bit of pent-up tension, I think. My thighs are knackered mind. I won't be able to walk for days.

*(**CARYL** and **MAX** take off their jackets and leave them in a heap on the floor with the oars.)*

*(**MEIRION** enters.)*

MEIRION. Well, I'm sure you'll both be relieved to hear that Ioan Lewis's kids have finally stopped crying.

CARYL. No one likes a poor loser.

SEREN. They're nine and seven!

MAX. Character building I'd say.

CARYL. My thoughts precisely. Bugger them. I've never felt so alive!

*(**MEIRION** walks over to the pile.)*

MEIRION. Well, you won't be *alive* if you break your neck on this lot. Give me a hand, will you?

(CARYL and MEIRION gather it all up to take into the back garden.)

SEREN. I can't believe you actually won.

MAX. Honestly, your mum was a machine. Just think, you'll be doing that with Beti in a few years.

SEREN. Don't know about that.

(SEREN takes Beti off her breast and puts her on her shoulder and gently pats her back.)

Mam and Dad are all tied up in knots about this new policy. Never seen them so stressed out. I'm still hoping they'll stay but I think they'll go. What are you going to do?

MAX. I'm not too worried. I bought this place with the inheritance money after my dad died. And I know I sound a bit, weird, but I just love being by the sea. I hate being away from it now. I get this ache you know.

SEREN. Well, Y Graith is lucky to have you.

MAX. You should come out with me one day, for a swim.

SEREN. Yeah, I'd like that.

(CARYL and MEIRION enter.)

MAX. Hey, Meirion, don't suppose you fancy a pint in The Ship do you, help me celebrate?

CARYL. Behave! Are we living in the 1950s still? Just the men that get to go to the pub, is it? Seren, is Beti done now?

SEREN. She's just drifting off now I think mam.

CARYL. So, Max, why don't you and Seren go down and we can follow with Beti when she wakes up?

SEREN. Oh no, Max probably wants / to

MAX. No! That would be lovely. If you want to?

SEREN. Do I want to go into a pub without my baby? Hold on. Let me think about that? Yes, Max. Yes, I do! You sure that's okay mam?

CARYL. I don't think she'll be any trouble and you're only over there.

SEREN. That's great, thank you.

> (**SEREN** *puts Beti in the cot.* **CARYL** *goes over and looks over Beti.*)

I'll just need to run upstairs and sort myself out. Shall I see you there in ten?

MAX. I'll get the drinks in. What do you fancy?

> (**SEREN** *heads off upstairs.*)

SEREN. Half a cider please. And a cheeky water chaser.

MAX. Right. See you over there.

> (**MAX** *leaves.*)

CARYL. Are you seeing what I'm seeing?

MEIRION. Don't get carried away Caryl.

CARYL. Just come here and look at this little girl.

> (**MEIRION** *joins* **CARYL** *by the cot.*)

That could be Seren. Don't you think? Takes me right back.

MEIRION. Caryl.

CARYL. New blood in the family. I can feel her Viking spirit. She's a fierce one.

MEIRION. You seem to have forgotten.

CARYL. I've not forgotten. Can't we just enjoy this moment? Having Beti here. Having Seren here. Having them both here with us.

MEIRION. My grandfather's eyes shone with pride over this house. A home for us all he'd say. And I've just destroyed that. Soon we'll all have to say goodbye, when *she's* only just arrived.

CARYL. But what if we don't?

MEIRION. I'm not a coward Caryl. We tell Seren tonight and on Monday morning I'm going to the police.

(A knock at the back door.)

GARETH. *(From outside.)* Hello. I need a hand here.

*(**CARYL** opens the door and **GARETH** enters carrying a cumbersome box. He is wearing shorts and a tee-shirt which reads: 'Porth Y Graith Annual Regatta' on the front, and 'Your Werth Properties. Because You Ar Werth It' on the back.)*

You forgot to collect your prize Mrs Hughes.

MEIRION. What's in there then?

GARETH. Meat. Three hundred pounds worth. Squids not ounces.

MEIRION. What are we going to do with all that?

GARETH. I suggest you stick it in the freezer as it has to be eaten by Monday.

CARYL. We've no room in the freezer.

GARETH. Right, well. Not really my look out.

*(**GARETH** puts it down on the table and straightens himself up.)*

But yeah, congratulations again Mrs Hughes. Very nice to see you getting into the spirit.

CARYL. I was coerced.

GARETH. I wish the same could be said for me, but I was a very willing participant of the crabbing competition.

CARYL. How many did you get?

GARETH. Not a single one. That'll teach me showing off to the new boyfriend. I did catch an eel though. Anyway, how are you two getting on?

MEIRION. Sorry?

GARETH. With the house? I've just managed to shift a couple of lovely properties in a little village like this up by Fishguard, similar predicament to you. Buyers don't seem to have caught on yet, won't be long though mind.

(**SEREN** *comes downstairs but stops on the bottom stairs, unseen, and listens.*)

MEIRION. We're still talking it through. Some stuff to sort out first. Anyway, decent thing you did today though, sponsoring the old regatta.

CARYL. I didn't realise I'd missed it so much.

GARETH. Well, you know. Good to give back. And I always loved spending the summers here with my uncle and his family when I was a kid. Such a lush village, but even better now that arsehole next door to you has gone. Ruined my cousin Nia's life he did.

SEREN. Nia Jenkins? From up the top, Pen Y Bryn, was it?

(*They all turn and look at* **SEREN**.)

GARETH. My dad's brother's daughter.

SEREN. You're her little cousin, aren't you?

GARETH. Gareth, yeah. Seren, right?

SEREN. Nia was what, two, maybe three years younger than me? We hung out a bit when we were kids. What did Glyn do to her?

GARETH. She was always so talented wasn't she, Nia. Glyn invited her over for some lessons, to help her with her painting technique apparently. My auntie and uncle were made up, *him* helping her out. But instead he ended up getting her pregnant, just before she turned seventeen.

CARYL. You're not serious? That's disgusting.

GARETH. It was horrible to tell you the truth. She said it was consensual, but I can't see how. Not really. But she begged her parents not to make a fuss. She didn't keep it. Didn't want to. And then they decided to sell up and go. See with him still knocking around, likely to stir up some trouble, they didn't want to stay.

(**CARYL** *takes the medal from round her neck. She is visibly shaken.*)

SEREN. I didn't know.

MEIRION. None of us knew.

GARETH. Villages like this, the beauty of them, they take your breath away, but scratch the surface and God only knows what you'll find. No offence like but I see it everywhere, in my game. Right, well, I've got a fresh pint waiting for me at The Ship, so I should scoot.

MEIRION. Mind how you go, and we'll be in touch soon.

GARETH. Tara then.

(**GARETH** *exits.*)

CARYL. Jesus. That's just. What a… Oh God, that poor girl. All that time. I never knew…

SEREN. Why didn't anyone stop him?

MEIRION. *Nobody* knew.

SEREN. How can you be so sure?

CARYL. Because if they did, he'd have been reported. Behaving like that. He deserved locking up. Jesus.

SEREN. But I knew.

MEIRION. What, love?

SEREN. I knew.

MEIRION. How could you know?

SEREN. I knew. And I could have stopped him.

CARYL. You knew?

SEREN. I could have stopped that from happening to Nia.

CARYL. What did you know?

SEREN. I thought it was just me.

MEIRION. What exactly are you saying?

SEREN. I'm just saying that I knew. I knew what he was capable of.

CARYL. How? How did you know?

SEREN. You always had such a soft spot for him, didn't you. You all did. Why?

MEIRION. Did that man do something to you?

SEREN. What if he did? He's gone now. And I hope to hell he never comes back.

MEIRION. What did he do?

SEREN. …

MEIRION. We're your parents, Seren.

SEREN. I just felt so embarrassed. And disgusted. And scared.

CARYL. Seren. You need to tell us.

SEREN. I had to go over there one day. I can't remember why. I went round the back, and he shouted down from his studio. Called me down to him.

CARYL. How old were you?

SEREN. Sixteen, just. He was covered in paint, his hands thick with the stuff and drinking Pernod. He gave me a glass of it. I stood there, a crab in one hand and a glass of Pernod in the other. *(Beat.)* That's what I was doing there, I had a crab for him. You'd sent me with a crab for him. But he didn't take it off me. He took out a cloth and cleaned his hands, telling me about this new picture he'd been working on. He used some turps to make sure he'd got all the paint off his hands. Meticulous, he was. Took ages. All the time going on about this painting, telling me how many shades of blue he'd used. Then he put the cloth down. I thought he was going to take it then. The crab. But then he came up close to me, his eyes, his dark eyes, fixed on me and then he just slowly stretched out his arm and he put his hand between my legs. He gripped. Hard. I had shorts on. And I should have done something, but I had both hands full. I froze. I couldn't understand what I was meant to do. What was I meant to do? I didn't know what to do. He didn't actually. I mean he did. But he didn't. But he wanted me to know that he could. Then suddenly he just took his hand away and smiled at me. Asked if I liked the painting. I spilled the Pernod everywhere and then I dropped the crab. As I left, he shouted "tell your dad, he owes me a fiver so that should just about cover it."

CARYL. I'm going to be sick.

SEREN. I can still taste the Pernod, even now. Why didn't I stop him? Why didn't anyone stop him?

CARYL. Your father did.

SEREN. What?

CARYL. Glyn didn't just disappear.

SEREN. Sorry, what?

MEIRION. Oh, Caryl!

CARYL. You were going to tell her today, anyway.

MEIRION. Not like this, Caryl.

CARYL. Are you telling her? Or am I?

MEIRION. We don't need to do this right now.

SEREN. What did you mean, he didn't just disappear? You can't just say that and then / expect

CARYL. Your father killed him. And if he hadn't, I'd be round there right now with a fucking carving knife. Tell her Meirion. Or I will.

SEREN. I think you better start talking dad.

MEIRION. When your mother was in hospital, Glyn came round here, and we got into a fight. He fell over the step. That bloody stupid step. And I don't know. The way he landed, it just killed him. I killed him.

SEREN. Jesus Christ. Is this a joke?

MEIRION. It was an accident.

SEREN. I don't know what I'm supposed to say to that. This is insane.

CARYL. He deserved it.

MEIRION. He was particularly well oiled, and he said some stuff about your mother, really nasty, horrid stuff, stuff that I just couldn't ignore. He wanted a rise out of me. I shouldn't have reacted. And I should have come clean at the time, but I panicked. I told your mother a few months back now. And we've agreed that I'm going to go to the police and confess.

CARYL. Have we hell agreed to it. You can count me out of that.

MEIRION. But I wanted to wait until I knew Beti was here safe and sound before.

SEREN. You're not serious? You can't do that.

MEIRION. I have to, love.

SEREN. Hold on. Where is he?

MEIRION. Glyn?

SEREN. Yes.

(**CARYL** *looks at* **MEIRION** *for a moment.*)

CARYL. He's buried under the shed, love.

(**SEREN** *starts laughing.*)

SEREN. No, he's not. No, he can't be. This is totally nuts! What the hell?! I mean, come on, this has to be some sort of sick wind up. As if you'd do that.

CARYL. I don't think your father was thinking straight.

SEREN. No! Who'd do that? Who the hell would do that?

MEIRION. It was winter, the village was totally empty. I didn't. I thought it was best to bury him here. Where I knew where he was.

SEREN. Okay, great, so you are actually serious.

MEIRION. I thought if I could keep him / here.

SEREN. Fuck! Sorry for swearing but Fuuuuuuck! Fuck, fuck, fuck. Like what the actual fuck. You fucking killed him dad. You actually killed him. You killed that evil little man.

(**SEREN** *suddenly resolute.*)

And nobody else knows? But you two? And now me? And no-one has ever suspected you or asked any questions?

MEIRION. I told the police that the last time I saw him, he was heading up the costal path.

SEREN. And nothing since?

(**MEIRION** *shakes his head.*)

Then there is absolutely no way, *no way*, that you're going to the police.

MEIRION. I have to, Seren. I won't let him do this to us anymore.

SEREN. Dad, you wouldn't survive for a minute in prison. It would kill you.

MEIRION. I have to do this.

SEREN. No. No, no you don't dad. In fact, you know what, you've done Porth Y Graith a favour, you've done the whole world a favour. How many more women, girls even, was he going to do that to? How many more lives would he ruin? If you go and confess, then what will that do to our family? What will that, what will that do to Beti? What will it do to this village? Don't go raising the dead dad. You bring that body up and innocent people's lives will be destroyed. And it's not as if anyone cares. Nobody is lying awake at night wondering what happened to Glyn. His sons couldn't give a shit. They've not been back here in years. Ask yourself what he was like with them behind closed doors. What did he do to *them* to make them stay away from here? He's missing but not missed. He ruined this place for me. He ruined more than that. Nobody, and I mean *nobody*, needs to know about what's out there. That's our secret. The three of us.

CARYL. You know she's right Meirion.

MEIRION. I can't, I don't want either of you implicated. If they find out that you knew, then we're all in trouble.

SEREN. You wouldn't stand a chance dad. They'd send you down for years.

CARYL. Meirion, please listen to Seren.

MEIRION. So, what do we do? What do I do? Tell me what I do.

SEREN. We do nothing.

CARYL. We stay here. Meirion. And we just carry on. We stay here. Bugger the money. We stay here in our home. This house has been in your family for seven generations. A few more generations and nobody will care.

MEIRION. But what if someone finds out?

SEREN. Nobody will find out. It's just another family secret. Every family has them. You know what dad, shit happens. And I'm sorry it happened to you, but it happened to me too and I'm sure mam's had her own share of shit over the years, but I will not let that destroy our family. I will not let that man's actions destroy my daughter's life. We're free of him. We should be celebrating! *(Beat.)* Oh bugger. Max will be in the pub by himself. I should go. I could do with a drink.

MEIRION. What? Now?

SEREN. Yes *now*. And come with Beti, when she wakes up, like we said.

MEIRION. You want me to come over to The Ship? Tonight?

SEREN. Honestly dad, fuck Glyn. You're the most beautiful man I know.

(Blackout.)

Scene Three

(The painting has been taken down and has been put aside in the room.)

MAX. I thought Ioan Lewis was going to ask me outside for a fight the way he was staring at me.

*(**MEIRION** and **SEREN** enter through the back door. **MEIRION** is carrying Beti in the car seat, he puts the car seat down on the table.)*

CARYL. Take no notice of Ioan Lewis. But tell me, more importantly, how did you enjoy your dance with Randy Rhiannon?

MAX. Thank you for saving me, Caryl.

CARYL. She loves a tourist. She'll be mortified when she realises you've bought down here, and she has to say hello to you all summer, every summer.

SEREN. No, you seem to be making yourself very at home here Max. Very popular. Chatting to everyone, you were.

MAX. Jenny always hated that about me.

CARYL. I could tell that when I met her. You were there asking us all sorts of questions and she just stood there staring at us with her mouth agog, like we were a photo in some holiday brochure. She was probably wondering why I didn't have a chimney pipe on my head. You're well shot love.

*(**CARYL** opens the box of meat to look inside.)*

I don't believe it. It's just burgers. All burgers. Oh no, hold on, there's some sausages too. 300 pounds of burgers and sausages to be eaten by Monday. Half of this is yours though mind, Max.

MAX. Barbeque on the beach for everyone? Tomorrow?

CARYL. We can't eat all this. My gallbladder won't take it.

SEREN. I think he means *everyone*, everyone.

MAX. Like the whole village everyone. I'm just on this WhatsApp group. Y Graith Together. Someone added me in the pub tonight. For people who want to share updates about the village.

CARYL. Like who?

MAX. Hold on. Let me just, finish this. "Spread the word. Plenty to go around. Caryl promises not to gloat. Bring your own drinks." There done it. Sent. Right, let's see. There's Branwen and Alun from The Ship, the Lewis clan, Catrin Jones, she's the one who added me.

CARYL. Oh, that sounds about right. She loves a *village update* that one.

MAX. Daf who runs the boats and the Griffiths family. Are they the ones with the llamas?

MEIRION. Different lot.

MAX. Then these I definitely don't know, Geraint Morgan.

CARYL. Big Ger!

SEREN. He's a funeral director from Newport way.

MEIRION. Has a chain of them.

SEREN. And his wife makes dresses out of flowers.

CARYL. No, no, I think he's got some new fancy woman now.

SEREN. Never!

MAX. Alys Parry?

CARYL. Now, she's tidy. School-teacher from Wrexham originally. But they live in London. The one with all the babies. Her husband is big in A.I.

MEIRION. *Was* big in A.I. Now he thinks the robots are coming to take over.

(**MAX**'s *phone beeps.*)

MAX. Oh, here we go, get in, Alun from The Ship says he's got a load of spare burger buns we can have, and he'll send over some complimentary condiments. And Jeremy and Claudia are in. Who are they?

CARYL. From Bath. House there. House here. House in Provence. Awful life.

MAX. Who else? Hold on. Stop the bus. Anthony Hopkins!

CARYL. Not Hannibal Lecter I'm afraid. Although he does have terrible red wine lips. Tony, bit of a pisshead, comes from near Stafford, I think.

MEIRION. And he's actually a vegan.

CARYL. Any more?

MAX. Just Rhiannon Richards. Is that Randy / Rhi?

CARYL. The good lady you met this evening. Is that it?

MAX. That is it.

(**CARYL** *looks out the window.*)

CARYL. All off to bed now. Off to their own little dreams of God knows what. I don't even want to imagine.

MAX. Well, bed for me too now. I'll dream of our victory Caryl. I'll come round in the morning and let you know final numbers.

CARYL. Nos Da Max. Do me a favour, add me to that group, that'll give them all a fright.

MEIRION. See you tomorrow, Max.

(**MEIRION** *gives* **MAX** *a man hug.*)

SEREN. Max, if it's okay, with you, I'd like to come over in the morning, see what you've done to the place.

MAX. Totally. I'll give you the grand tour. You'll hardly recognise it. Don't forget to bring Beti though, I think she'll really dig my reclaimed wood kitchen cabinets with soft-close drawers. A thing of beauty.

> (**MAX** *walks over to Beti and hangs his medal over her car seat.*)

This is for you. Nos da little cabbage.

> (**MAX** *exits.* **SEREN** *picks up the car seat and heads for the stairs.*)

SEREN. I'll head up now, one last feed for Beti and then I'll try and get a bit of sleep.

MEIRION. Seren, can I just say again, how sorry I am to have let you down / like

SEREN. Don't start that now. It's a fresh start dad. A fresh start, here, at home. And look, I promise I'll come down more often to stay.

CARYL. Max will be pleased!

SEREN. Bloody hell mam. Do you ever stop? Maybe you could try, occasionally, just when you're about to say something, something you probably shouldn't, just stop and think.

CARYL. But where would the fun be in that then?

SEREN. No, you're probably right. *(Beat.)* What was it that Glyn said? About you? That made Dad so angry?

MEIRION. Save that for another day, eh?

SEREN. Fair enough. I'm about to drop.

> (**SEREN** *heads for the stairs.*)

CARYL. Wake me first thing and I'll take over so you can go back to bed for a bit, okay?

SEREN. Thanks mam.

(She disappears up the stairs.)

*(**CARYL** picks up the picture.)*

CARYL. What shall I do with this then?

MEIRION. That's up to you Caryl.

CARYL. I can't keep it, not *now*. I thought I could. That she was more me than him. But I look at her now and it's like looking at a stranger. Someone I sort of recognise but not quite. Someone I met on holiday once perhaps. Making a fool of herself. Or maybe I know exactly who she is, and I just don't like her very much. *(Beat.)* When we were in the Ship tonight, I looked at them all. All of them down here, having such a great time, enjoying their *other* lives. And I'm no better than any of them, am I? Doing what I wanted, taking what I wanted, regardless of the consequences, no matter who it affected or who it hurt. *(Beat.)* How didn't I realise who he was? How didn't I realise who I was? *(Beat.)* No, I'll be glad to say goodbye.

MEIRION. It's just a painting, Caryl.

*(**CARYL** smiles and nods.)*

CARYL. I'll stick it in the shed, and we can burn it in the fire once it gets cold again. Keep us warm.

*(**CARYL** takes the picture out to the shed.)*

*(**MEIRION** starts to look for something but stops to look at the photo of his grandparents and smiles.)*

*(**CARYL** re-enters.)*

CARYL. That's better. Just us again.

(**MEIRION** *walks over to* **CARYL**.)

MEIRION. Give us a kiss, Caryl Hughes.

(**MEIRION** *takes* **CARYL** *in his arms and kisses her before staring into her eyes.*)

CARYL. You okay, Meirion?

MEIRION. Funny how these things work out.

CARYL. I don't pretend to understand the mysteries of the universe, Meirion.

MEIRION. I don't pretend to understand the mysteries of you, Caryl.

CARYL. No?

MEIRION. But I wouldn't mind having a look at them later.

(*They kiss again.*)

Have you seen my Fishing Monthly anywhere?

(**CARYL** *finds it for him.*)

CARYL. Here you go.

MEIRION. Thought I'd have a quick flick through before bed. Get me in the mood.

(**MEIRION** *heads off upstairs.*)

CARYL. I'll turn everything off and be up in a minute.

MEIRION. Don't be long.

(**CARYL** *moves around the room turning off lights and getting ready to go to bed. With the room in darkness,* **CARYL** *heads up the stairs but stops halfway up.*)

CARYL. The bloody meat!

> (**CARYL** *comes back down into the kitchen and opens the box and pulls out some burgers. She opens the fridge door. Light from the fridge illuminates a section of the room. The back door creaks open to reveal* **GLYN**, *covered in mud. He wolf-whistles.)*

> (**CARYL** *turns and, upon seeing* **GLYN**, *gives a little yelp before steadying herself. She looks at him for a second.)*

Right. I thought that might have been you, getting soil all over my floor. Before you start, I've heard about you and your disgusting persuasions. If I'd have known what you were up to. If I'd have known that you dared touch my daughter. I'd have killed you myself. And it would have hurt a hell of a lot more. Well, this is our house and you are very, *very* far from welcome here. Now, I'm going back upstairs, back to my husband, and *you*, you filthy old bastard, you can bugger off back outside, back in the dirt, back where you belong.

(Blackout.)

End

Milton Keynes UK
Ingram Content Group UK Ltd.
UKHW050730260324
439885UK00001B/1